TH

THE GIFT
OF FEELING

Paul Tournier

SCM PRESS LTD

Translated by Edwin Hudson from the French
La mission de la femme
Delachaux et Niestlé, Neuchâtel and Paris 1979

© Delachaux et Niestlé 1979
Translation © Edwin Hudson 1981

253.5

20029890

334 02023 9
First published in English 1981
by SCM Press Ltd
58 Bloomsbury Street, London WC1

Photoset by John Smith, London
and printed in Great Britain by
Richard Clay (The Chaucer Press) Ltd
Bungay, Suffolk

Contents

1

Objective Relationship and Personal Relationship

I believe that women have a mission today. Men have kept them out of public life and have built up our Western technical civilization without them – a masculine society, ordered entirely in accordance with masculine values, and tragically lacking the contribution women could make.

Before tackling the problem of the role of women in the world, I shall say something of my own life, my childhood and youth, which I have often mentioned in my lectures, but seldom written about in my books. This is in order that the reader may follow me step by step in my personal experiences and better understand why they have instilled in me this idea that women have an important role of their own to play.

My father was born in 1828, in the same year as Henri Dunant, the founder of the Red Cross, and, I believe, in the same district of Geneva, the old town. So he would be one hundred and fifty now, since I write these lines in 1978. He was seventy when I was born, and as I am now eighty, that makes the hundred and fifty.

Recently I met an old lady who lived in the house where I was born. She was then a little girl of eight, and had been allowed to come up to our flat to see me that very day. She told me that what she specially remembered was the wild joy of my father at having a son at his age.

My father died two months later. You can imagine how attached my mother must have been to me, the tiny little baby boy left with her by her old husband; and how attached I on my part must have been to her. I did indeed have a sister four years older, but she may well have felt jealous of my mother's favouritism of me.

A further complication was that at the age of six months I had a serious illness. Later on I made the acquaintance of the paediatrician who had looked after me. One day he took me into his study to show me my record card, on which he had written, 'No hope for this child.' Fortunately an old professor had suggested feeding me on ass's milk. A she-ass was at once procured, to the great pleasure of my sister, who was able to have donkey rides round the orchard: a nice way of getting her own back! So I owe my life to medicine, even though the means at its command were less powerful then than they are today, and to an ass, the most biblical of animals.

However, when I was six my mother died after a long illness and several operations. My sister and I were taken into their home by an uncle and aunt who brought us up with the greatest devotion. I must here pay them this tribute, especially my uncle, who respected my position, never letting me forget that I was not his son, and that I must be myself, the son of my father. Thus, when I informed him that I was planning to marry, he replied: 'I have nothing to say to you. Think, and ask yourself what your father would think about it.'

I have therefore no complaint against those who brought me up with so much affection. Nevertheless the decisive thing for a child is what he himself feels. When my mother died I felt lost and in the dark. I felt that I no longer mattered to anyone. I can hardly remember my mother, which is not normal, since I was already six years old. The happy memories of the past have probably been repressed along with the distress I felt, leaving only the sense of void. I became turned in upon myself, solitary, shy, unsociable, incapable of forming relationships with others of my age.

I preferred to climb up into a tree, there to create my own isolated little world, or else I confided my secrets to my uncles' hunting dogs. My performance at school was mediocre. At that time the part played by emotional factors in child development was unrecognized, and failure at school was attributed only to idleness or stupidity. I do not believe that I was lazy, however.

We know, moreover, how impersonal school can be for the poorly adjusted child. It was much later, when I was sixteen, that one of my teachers, my classics master, realized my distress and made an unprecedented gesture designed to break down the psychological wall behind which I was hiding: he invited me to his home. How overawed I felt as I entered that austere study, its walls covered with bookshelves from floor to ceiling! I did not know what to say; and I thought afterwards that my teacher must have been embarrassed too.

At any rate, a relationship was gradually built up between us. Someone was listening to me, not as a pupil being questioned, but as a human being, a person. He was taking an interest in me, giving me the opportunity to express myself, to discover myself through expressing myself. Long afterwards I realized that for me he had been a psychotherapist. I went on visiting him every week for some years, when I was no longer his pupil.

The effect was magical. The very next year I organized my class into a society, and was elected its president. We had all sorts of interesting debates. It was the period of the First World War. Switzerland was divided between the sympathy of our northern cantons with Germany and our own with Belgium under the invader, and with France. Then we had theatrical evenings, one of which, with the assistance of my teacher friend, consisted of an act from a play be Euripides, in Greek, one from Plautus in Latin, and one from Molière in French. Soon I was engaged with a friend in writing a historical play about Nicolas de Flüe, the man who brought peace to Switzerland.

In this way there opened for me a period of social action and of intellectual and political debate, that was to last for a good number of years. The Russian revolution had taken place, arousing disturbances in defeated Germany, with repercussions in Switzerland, particularly among students. I soon found myself chairman of the principal student society, just then celebrating its centenary, involving important speeches in Lausanne, Zürich, and Lucerne. At the same time I was busy founding the Students' Union in the University of Geneva.

Then I was off to Vienna on behalf of the International Committee of the Red Cross, for the repatriation of Russian, Austrian, and German prisoners of war. Next came international aid for children, notably during a famine in the Volga Basin, and the creation of an international secretariat for youth movements dedicated to children's aid. In Geneva, the foundation of a Preventorium for infants whose mothers were suffering from tuberculosis. Lastly the church: I became a member of the Consistory, its governing body, as a representative of the 'Worried Sons of the Church', as we were called, a group of young lay people and theologians who wished to revive its fervour and faith. I was an enthusiastic Calvinist, and spoke out on the side of orthodoxy against modernism.

It was all done with a zeal and sincerity which I do not repudiate, but which occasioned more division than edification in the church. And so I felt a certain unease which I could not understand. It was then that I met my second psychotherapist, a Dutch financial expert

3

who held high office in the League of Nations. He too, like my classics master, invited me into his home. I was then thirty-four.

My new friend had been won over to a religious movement which was affecting me also, founded by the American pastor Frank Buchman, and which went under the name of the Oxford Group, because it was among the students of that university that he had begun his mission. It was a movement which put the accent not on dogma and theology, but on concrete obedience to God's inspiration in daily life, both private and public. They practised personal witness and what they called 'sharing', complete frankness with one another.

Thus, when I visited him my host spoke about his own intimate life with a simplicity and courage that I had never met before. When he finished I really felt that I could not talk to him about my activities (as I have just done here) but about myself, about my personal life. It was the first time I had ever put into words what I had suffered in being an orphan, and I was in tears as I did so.

My dialogue with the classics master had been altogether intellectual. I did indeed know something of his life, that he had been divorced and remarried, but it was from hearsay. He had never talked to me about it himself. I too expressed only ideas, never feelings. We were able to talk about my religious difficulties, but only on a philosophical level. I was a Christian, he a spiritualist. He believed in a universal Spirit, but not in a personal God. Neither he nor I suspected at that time that that personal God had used him to make me take a first step out of my solitude.

Now my Dutch friend was making me take a second. I was discovering a new kind of dialogue – the truly personal, emotional dialogue. During all those years of argument and action I had remained at bottom, without knowing it, a recluse at heart. Once in the early hours of the morning as I was leaving an enjoyable students' meeting, a fellow student came up to me on the pavement and said kindly, 'I've heard that you were an orphan.' At once I felt that well-known lump in the throat, and for fear of betraying my emotion and bursting into tears, I walked quickly away into the night without saying a word in reply.

One can make speeches before great crowds, give lectures, take part in public life, without revealing anything of oneself. You see, there are two modes of relationship with others: an intellectual and objective mode, and an emotional and personal mode. I have often spoken of two levels of dialogue, one superficial and the other profound. But it seems to me now that it would be better to speak of two poles. For the dialogue of ideas has its own importance, it can be profound, arising out of the fundamental beliefs of the participants. There are no grounds for declaring one of these modes of relationship superior to the other; they are simply different and complementary.

So there it is: it happens that, separated by an interval of almost twenty years, I had decisive, exemplary experiences, of the one kind with the classics master, and of the other with the Dutchman. They were quite distinct, but both of them as clear and convincing as laboratory experiments. That is why a friend advised me to begin my book with this account of my own life. For these two modes of relationship correspond respectively to the dominant qualities of man and of woman, the objective relationship to the rational tendency of the man, and the personal relationship to the affective tendency of the woman.

Now you cannot but be aware that we are taught the objective relationship from infant school onwards; that it dominates our conception of the world and of life, not only in the natural sciences, but also in the economic and social sciences and the humanities; that it is the universal norm, recognized in every domain. Whereas the personal relationship is extremely rare, and its value neglected. So that men find themselves at home in this rational society; they are scarcely even aware of what it lacks. Women, on the other hand, experience a vague unease. Their emotional life and their need of personal contact are left unsatisfied.

Women are of course capable of adapting to this masculine world. They have shown this clearly during the course of this century, and can today occupy with efficiency posts that once were the preserve of men. But that does not solve the problem. It is not by developing only their masculine aptitudes that women can find fulfilment, but by reintroducing into our modern Western civilization the personal relationship which it lacks. But it is not easy, in the atmosphere of objectivity which characterizes our civilization, to make the leap into the other attitude, that of personal commitment.

I made that leap, as if in spite of myself, at the age of thirty-four. I swung suddenly from one pole to the other. I swung too far, as swings are apt to do; I realize that well enough now. I was discovering the personal mode of relationship, and finding out how fruitful it is for oneself and for the other person, and how it helps to bind us together, so that we open our hearts to each other on what we have lived and felt, and no longer only on what we have read in books or learnt at school or from our own intellectual speculations.

I was discovering a new and moving contact with others: with my wife Nelly first of all. We understood and loved each other. But until then I had been, as she said at the time, a teacher rather than a husband; a teacher, a psychologist, even a pastor, always wanting to instruct her and explain everything to her intellectually, not seeing that so far as real personal relationship was concerned I had everything to learn. And so she soon became my third psychotherapist and my confessor. My relationship with my children and with my friends was also becoming richer; and finally with my patients, and that transformed my professional career.

My relationship with God was becoming quite different. Until then religion had been first and foremost a matter of ideas, correct or incorrect ideas about God, about Jesus, about man – in short, doctrines. I was learning to meditate, to listen to God, to meet him as a person, and to deepen my intimacy with him. Now at last I was discovering how lacking in charity I had been in all kinds of partisan arguments.

Next I had to make a series of visits to former adversaries, to ask their forgiveness.

To an old pastor whom I had criticized harshly; then, and especially, to my own pastor, who had been my father's successor, and who had kept a watching brief over me during my youth, as the orphan child of his master. In the circumstances we ought to have kept close to one another, the more so as our theological convictions were alike.

But the fact was that when we were together in the Consistory, we represented two differing tendencies – he, tradition and caution, and I, change and audacity. We had clashed like the leaders of two opposing political parties. We found ourselves on our knees in his study, praying together to ask God's forgiveness.

What I found even more surprising was that other former adversaries came to me on their own initiative, to ask for my help with their personal problems. All I had been interested in was combating their theological ideas, without any regard for them as persons. And here they were unveiling their persons before me, revealing their sufferings, their intimate conflicts, their secret dramas, which they had previously kept hidden, as I had hidden my own, behind the facade of intellectual argument.

All at once they were becoming my friends. I shared their

anxieties and understood why they acted as they did. And they had confidence in me. My new experiences had awakened in them the hope of finding in me the help they had failed to find elsewhere. I discovered how lonely they were. I measured then how wide is the gap for everybody between intellectual relationship and personal relationship.

Nevertheless, there is a link between our ideas and our personal problems, a link of which we are generally unconscious, and of which others are unaware, so long as we do not open our hearts to them about our emotional life. Ideas are impersonal, they are things that can be played with or traded like merchandise. We can use them as ammunition in the battle of life. And we remain alone so long as we do not find another mode of relationship with others.

2

The World of Things and the World of Persons

These two poles, these two widely differing modes of relationship with others and with the world, are described in a notable book by Martin Buber. He expresses them in two striking formulae: 'I-it' and 'I-thou'. The 'I' is common, it is myself.

In the 'I-it' relationship I am a cold, neutral observer, unengaged emotionally, as objective as possible. I do my utmost to suppress my personal feelings, as Descartes required, standing firmly on the ground of reason and commonsense, which that founder of modern thought claimed were alone shared by all men. Then everything I observe, including man, becomes an object to me, a thing.

That is the scientific attitude.

In the 'I-thou' relationship, on the other hand, I am concerned personally. There is no longer any question of my being neutral and impassive. It is no longer a question of observing, analysing, studying, making moral judgments or psychological diagnoses. It is no longer a question of knowledge mediated through intellectual concepts or technical instruments, but of immediate and reciprocal knowledge, in which I am myself committed, known by the other as well as I know him.

Martin Buber uses the example of a tree. He can study it as a botanist, label it, classify it according to its species, or describe its anatomy, its physiology, the strange physiological force which makes the sap rise, the even more marvellous chemical reactions that are involved, and which provide for us the oxygen we need. He can go on making such observations *ad infinitum*. But he can also talk to the tree, pay attention to its own voice, to what that tree signifies and expresses for him.

I once heard a psychoanalyst talking about her childhood, with experiences similar to mine. There was a tree to which she went each evening to recount her day, with its joys and its pains. Her tree listened to it all, sharing all of her life. Obviously, it was no longer a thing to her, but a living being – and more, a person, almost a mother to console her.

Martin Buber took the example of a tree, I suppose, in order to show us that the 'I-thou' relationship is not established only with human beings. When St Francis of Assisi addressed to 'brother sun' his well-known hymn, it was not the sun of the astronomers, the scientists who investigate its physical and chemical nature and its course in space. St Francis spoke to it as to a brother, a 'thou', a person.

Poets, too, fall in love with the moon as with a woman. And to the child his favourite teddy bear is not just a thing, but a person. He gives it a pet name, holds long and intimate conversations with it, shares all his secrets with it, kisses it and accepts its caresses as he strokes his cheek against its fur. You may say with the Freudians that he is making it the object of his libido, that is to say that his relationship with his teddy is no longer one of intellectual knowledge, but is a commitment of love.

It is not of course only with a teddy bear, the image of a living animal, that the child reveals his capacity to personify all he touches. The smallest object can take on this personal character. There is that well-known passage where Freud describes a child playing with a cotton-reel, hiding it and retrieving it again and again. Suddenly Freud realizes that the child is seeking in this way to accustom himself to his mother's absences. The reel is no longer a thing; it has become a person – his mother.

There is one detail that touches me personally in the story of Martin Buber. It is mentioned by André Haynal in his study of the meaning of despair. Martin Buber's parents were divorced when he was two years old, and he was brought up by his paternal grandparents. He was thus separated from his mother at a younger age even than I was. Dr Haynal thinks that the famous 'I-it', 'I-thou' formula could have been suggested to the philosopher by his missing his mother. It is not surprising that I feel so close to Martin Buber.

He is careful to warn us that the 'I-thou' relationship is never durable. Inevitably we are quick to readopt our attitude of objective observer with regard to the other person. So, when my former opponents came back to me to ask for help in their personal difficulties, I had of course to call upon my scientific, medical, and psychological knowledge. My sympathy did not suffice. What had changed was the emotional climate of our relationship. The two modes of relationship, objective and personal, are thus not in opposition: they are complementary. Nevertheless, however fleeting the moments of personal communion, they are the most important and fruitful moments of our lives. This is especially true of the personal encounter with God, which is usually felt only as an exceptional experience, a bolt from the blue, but which changes our lives altogether.

So this capacity for personal relationship is characteristic of human nature, and is in fact what makes it human. According to our state of mind all sorts of things can become persons for us, the entire world can be filled with persons. It is still the same world; it does not change. It is I who change my outlook on the world, my personal or impersonal attitude towards others. Turn and turn about, the world appears to me as a world of things or a world of persons.

For if we personify things, we can also reify persons. The word 'reify' is too learned, and I prefer Péguy's familiar expression '*chosifier*' (lit. 'thingify'). Already at the beginning of this century Péguy was denouncing the tendency to treat men as things as one of the most dangerous in our Western civilization. What would he be saying today? The triumph of science and technology, the automation of production, the bureaucratic centralization of the state, even leisure mass-produced, all are taking us more and more rapidly into a world of things, and into the eclipse of the person.

It was above all the influence of Péguy that prompted Emmanuel Mounier to conceive and found his Personalist Movement, and his review *Esprit*. Their warning cry was scarcely heard at all. And it was not the first. Karl Marx had already seen that industrialization was reducing the members of the proletariat to the status of mere things, in defiance of their status as persons. Pastor Fuchs finds it possible to write: 'Long before Marx, the Old Testament denounced the danger of treating persons as things.'

In the modern West it is not only the proletariat, but the managerial class, at the very top of the hierarchy of the 'consumer society', who feel themselves reduced to the status of things, instruments of production, interchangeable and impersonal cogs in an enormous machine which functions inexorably and blindly. Even artists – Régine Pernoud makes the point that financial speculation is transforming the work of art into an 'object' of art.

It is very difficult for us to perceive the things that are conditioning us, so that we do not realize the extent to which we are impregnated with this impersonal view of the world. It is suggested to us at school. From nursery school to university we are taught to adopt the scientific attitude; but science by definition knows only the world of things. Nature, history, society even, are seen as an endless round of phenomena which are rigorously linked in a chain of cause and effect. It is just an enormous mechanism in which we are inexorably caught, a sort of merry-go-round which gets us nowhere. For in the eyes of science nothing has meaning, since everything happens automatically at the whim of chance and necessity, as Jacques Monod has said.

How different from the schools of antiquity whose preoccupation was to teach children the myths, legends, and epics, from which they learned the meaning of life. The forces of nature, and human passions, were personified in the form of gods and heroes. Of course the children of Israel, the chosen people, fought against the polytheism of surrounding nations, even to the point of calling the sun and moon the 'greater and smaller lights' (Gen. 1.16), for fear that if they were designated by their names people might be tempted to worship them. However, it was really in order to proclaim that the one God was not an abstract principle, but a person, the 'living God', who gave meaning to creation.

Today, in an age when only science is believed in, even theologians are careful to cut a figure as objective scientists, and want to demythologize the Bible. This is happening at the same time as other scientists, the psychoanalysts, are revealing to us that man is not governed by reason but by myths, and if the myths of revealed religion are taken away from him he will invent other, very dangerous ones, such as the myth of technical progress, or the myth of racism.

However, it is not at all my intention to write a pamphlet against science. I am a man of science, and I recognize its merits without reservation. It is foolish to denigrate it. In the intellectual sphere, for the comprehension of nature and of man, its value is impressive. In economic life it has procured, at least for some privileged countries, (and somewhat to the detriment of the others) very considerable prosperity. In medicine alone it has made possible enormous advances.

For this it has indeed been necessary to study man as if he were a thing! The anatomy laboratory is the student's first initiation into medicine, and always an overwhelming experience for him. He simply has to learn to overcome his squeamishness, to forget that that corpse has been a person's body, to learn to dissect it like

11

carving wood or stone. The same is true in his clinical studies, and even in psychology. Throughout he will be taught, in the interest of the patients themselves, to keep a cool head, to set aside his feelings, and to remain objective.

That is why a doctor can make the silliest mistakes in diagnosis when it is his own wife or children he is treating, as has happened in my own case. He has in such cases to defer to colleagues who will be able at once to see things to which his feelings have blinded him.

On the other hand the most scientific of doctors, men like Eric Martin, for example, remind us continually that when it comes to treatment, patients can no longer be treated as things, or with the lack of respect which we feel appropriate in handling things. And that the patient has as much need of his doctor's personal contact as of his scientific knowledge.

The medicine of the person is not a 'marginal' medicine like antipsychiatry or other doctrines that are critical of academic science. You see, once again we are not concerned with inclining too much to one or other of the two opposite poles, but with discovering the many-faceted interplay of their complementarity. What is wrong is the imbalance; we suffer from the predominance of things over persons, so that our technological civilization seems inhuman, and man no more than an object.

And what about woman? The fact is that she has been treated as a thing even more than men have. First, as a servant. Poor thing, she has so often been condemned to 'live through a third party, through a man'; deprived of any right to a personal existence; bound to the service of others – to parents, to brothers and sisters, and then to a selfish husband, or to an employer who underestimates her work. In many parts of the world it is in their role as servants that women are still looked upon as the property of their husbands when married, and are even more despised when they are not. Things can be possessed, but not persons.

Next, as a sexual 'object'. Man is specifically a voyeur; but what he sees is not persons, but things. The present wave of pornography is an extreme illustration of the primacy of things over persons. A sympathetic feminist like Marie Cardinal, despite the liberation which she has achieved through Freudian psychoanalysis, tells us how fed up she is with the atmosphere of sex-appeal in which women are portrayed only as things to excite desire.

Another feminist, Michèle Perrein, still in a distraught state, tells her friend Denis, with whom she has lived for a long time, that she has been assaulted in the street, that she has had to defend herself and escaped only with great difficulty. But Denis tells her that it is perfectly natural! Then she explodes: 'A thing, that's what I was in the street, and a thing was what I was at home, since Denis found it quite normal.' Thereupon she breaks with Denis in order to become a person again.

Our scientific world reduces even love to a technique. We see young girls reading massive books on the physiology of sex, and no doubt they could recite a list of the erogenous zones, but no one has told them that for the enjoyment of sex the abandonment of person to person is more important than any artifice.

Lastly, women are turned into things by being treated as ornaments, as decoration, as a means of supplying charm or prestige. You know the society formula, 'Look pretty and keep your mouth shut.' The Abbé Oraison writes, 'I cannot accept a culture in which woman's place is as an object of use, of luxury, or amusement.'

There are then two complementary poles, the taste for things and the sense of the person, between which a just balance must be re-established in our civilization. They more or less correspond to the complementarity between man and woman with which I wish to deal in this book. I say 'more or less', because it is understood that there is masculine and feminine in every human being, whether man or woman. There are men who have this sense of the person, and women whose bent is towards technology and things. The complementarity of the sexes is not only an external matter between men and women, but also internal, between the two tendencies which are present in each of us.

I am here evoking orientations, mentalities, rather than precise concepts. I am employing terms such as things and persons, men and women, as symbols perceived intuitively rather than through rigorous and conceptual thought. They are symbols which always go in pairs, each evoking the other.

Take as an example Pascal's 'spirit of geometry' and 'spirit of finesse'. Men like geometry – it is precise and measurable. They judge the value of a sportsman to the hundredth of a second, for there is no more irrefutable proof than figures. Women will make up their minds rather on the attractiveness of his style. Men are more attached to quantity, women to quality.

Anaïs Nin sees the contrast between men and women as being like that between intellectual thought and poetry. C.G. Jung too places intellect and feeling at the two poles of one axis, one predominating in men, the other in women. I could give other examples of these complementary poles – objectivity and subjectivity, logic and intuition, mechanism and life. Or again, the polarity between realism and symbolism, between the utilitarian and the pleasurable, between industrialism and ecology, the distance that lies between doing and being, the gulf between physics and metaphysics, the opposition between technology and the humanities.

When I was in the academic section at secondary school, for the first time a girl was admitted to the class I was in. At first we looked upon her with some irony, but soon with a certain chagrin, because she was doing well. Since that time it has become commonplace for girls to enter the academic section, while boys have tended to move on to the technical side. Today, writes Kate Millett, 'the humanities, because not exclusively male, suffer in prestige'.

Nevertheless it was philosophy which proclaimed with Descartes the primacy of rational and scientific thought over sensibility and feeling. There is a delightful chapter on Descartes in a book by Annie Leclerc. She ought to know what she is talking about, since she is a teacher of philosophy. She admits to the voluptuous pleasure she has in reading him. But she enjoys it as a spectacle, as she might enjoy an act by a clever conjuror, without believing one word of what he says. Quite the contrary, since he rejects feelings in favour of reason. And she concludes, maliciously, 'What is the use of philosophy? ... For pleasure.' That is a nice turning of the tables by a woman on three centuries of rationalism! We shall find this term 'pleasure' recurring frequently in her writing.

Men love grand, abstract, universal theories. Women are more attached to the details of experience. Men like dirt and disorder, women like cleaning and tidying. Men doubt everything, women believe everything. Men take everything lightly, women take everything seriously. Am I joking, man that I am? – Of course! But who does not see, or rather feel, the malaise of our Western civilization? That it has ended up by tipping right over on the side it leaned towards – the side of things? That men take greater pleasure than women in counting, measuring, weighing, manipulating, combining and amassing in order to increase their power?

This movement culminated in the nineteenth century – 'the stupid century' according to Léon Daudet whom we read enthusiastically when we were students – with its positivist philosophy which set the seal on the primacy of the rational disciplines; with its industrial revolution which had no criterion but that of production at any price; with its colonialism and its racism; and, in medicine, with Virchow and an exclusively anatomical and physiological interpretation of disease.

I have already spoken of Martin Buber and the world of things, a long time ago, in my book *The Meaning of Persons.* At that time I had not yet noticed that the loss of a sense of the person in our modern civilization coincided with the rejection of women into the intimacy of the home and their exclusion from political, economic, and cultural life. It was the nineteenth century also which saw the culmination of this eviction of women. Consider the preamble of the Code Napoléon, quoted by Gisèle Halimi: 'Woman is given to man for the purpose of producing children. She is therefore his property, as the fruit-tree is the property of the gardener.'

There you have her juridical inferiority. As for her economic inferiority, this also arose out of the industrial revolution, which deprived her of the considerable role she had played until then in production. Finally it was to the nineteenth century also that Victorianism belonged, with its puritanism and the sexual taboos which Freud was to turn upside down, and its view of women as dangerous temptresses turning man away from the path along which reason alone ought to lead him.

3

Western Civilization since the Renaissance

I am quite convinced now that this historical coincidence is not fortuitous. 'Western culture,' writes Karlfried Dürckheim, 'is in essence masculine. From the unilateral development of manly qualities there results the lack of recognition, if not the repression, of feminine potentialities.' And the converse is no less evident: because women have been kept in the background, because they have scarcely played any part at all in its evolution, Western culture has been orientated towards masculine values – power, reason, technology. Men have constructed a society of things because they alone were concerned in the work of construction.

There is, then, a double movement. Two relationships of cause and effect overlap and form a vicious circle. They have been re-inforcing each other throughout the present era: a society devoted to masculine values despises and rejects woman; and a society in which woman no longer exercises any influence orders itself increasingly in accordance with those masculine values.

Perhaps you will tell me that there was no real choice at the beginning of this process, that necessity, or political and especially economic pressures, orientated the West in this direction. That is not true. The Renaissance made a resolute choice of the rational as against the irrational, of the 'I-it' as against the 'I-thou', of objectivity as against affective and mystical communion, of physics against metaphysics. Western man has indeed got the world he wanted.

Denis de Rougemont has clearly demonstrated the primacy of voluntary choices over the determinism of economic needs, showing that man is much more responsible than he believes for what becomes of him. De Rougemont takes a quite recent example, the motor car, which in the course of this century has completely transformed the economic system, caused the present energy crisis, and brought intractable problems to our cities and our whole environment; and now we cannot do without it.

All this is because Henry Ford had the idea of manufacturing cars at a time when, according to his own admission, no one wanted to buy them. The most difficult thing therefore was not to manufacture them, but to persuade people to buy them – to create a need. Technology was no use without propaganda. Ford chose as the theme of his publicity the idea of pure air: 'The automobile will enable you to escape from the polluted air of the cities, to breathe the pure air of the countryside.' He did not foresee that cars would be used more in towns than in the country, and would poison the atmosphere in the towns more than ever.

The truth is that man has never done anything but what he wanted to do, and what he has wanted to do has always been suggested to him by those who have been the masters of his thoughts. Since the Renaissance these masters have been telling him – with many variations, to be sure, but with a growing assurance – what you well know:

That the old idea of a God who created the universe and gave it its laws, who created man, breathed his Spirit into him, giving him a measure of liberty but claiming obedience from him; who himself broke into history to save him from the unhappy consequences of his disobedience ... that all this is a beautiful story – naïve, poetic, edifying – but invented by men in an age of ignorance; a myth, like the legends that have always been invented by men to console themselves for their impotence in the face of nature and destiny; but that such stories can be seen now as merely the vestiges of a religious phase in the development of man, an age now gone by, since science by means of objective study is bringing us true knowledge.

Furthermore, that man ought now to rely only on himself, on his reason and his creative genius, on his science and technology, the only source of all possible progress; that he ought to make history instead of submitting to it; that it is he who freely chooses his values, and he ought to have the courage to assume them; that nothing is sacred, nothing is taboo; and that fancies, tenderness, sentiment – all of them dear to women – can very well be left to the intimacy of his private life at home, but that in the conduct of society, in his political, economic, and professional life, he ought not to be uncumbered with such things, since all that matters there is the law of the strongest and the will to power.

As you see, there is a parallel between this evolution of thought

17

since the Renaissance and the banishment of women into private life. This banishment, which has been characteristic of society during the last four centuries, has been accompanied in the minds of men themselves by the repression of the tendencies which are symbolized by women: sentiment, personal relationship, emotional and affective life, devotion, self-sacrifice, modesty, and gentleness.

The fact is that the complementarity of the sexes is more than an external harmony between two distinct beings, man and woman, in marriage and in their social relationships. It is also an interior harmony within each of us, both men and women, between our masculine and our feminine tendencies. This double harmony is symbolized by the well-known Chinese Yin-Yang sign:

C.G. Jung uses the term *animus* for the masculine tendency present in the mind of the woman, and *anima* for the feminine tendency present in that of the man.

In order to affirm his virility man represses to some extent his *anima*, and conversely. I say 'to some extent', because over-radical repression makes both men and women incomplete, disharmonious, amputated beings. This is what has happened since the Renaissance, and what our civilization is suffering from. Now woman is – sometimes too violently – liberating her *animus*. But she can also help man to liberate his *anima*. I think this is what has happened in my own case: I often feel myself a mother as well as a father to my patients.

Freud, on the other hand, protested sharply when Hilda Doolittle told him she found a mother in him: 'I must tell you,' he asserts, '(you were frank with me, and I will be frank with you), I do not like to be the mother in transference – it always surprises and shocks me a little. I feel so very masculine.' Note in passing that in his concern for frankness Freud was not at that point as neutral and impersonal as his disciples sometimes claim.

However, I think that the reason for Freud's reaction was that he was a pioneer in his time, a time which saw the apogee of rationalism: he had to defend himself against the accusation by official medicine that his work was unscientific; and in order to achieve acceptance he had to affirm his masculine objectivity. But

18

he had a tenderness and also an artistic sensibility which had not escaped an exquisite woman poet like Hilda Doolittle, when he had shown her his fine collection of Egyptian and Greek statuettes.

It was indeed he who 'reintroduced subjectivity into medicine', in Viktor von Weizsäcker's words. Is not subjectivity the feminine principle – affectivity and a sense of the person? It was a great event, the first break in the system that had prevailed since the Renaissance, and especially since Descartes, based on the assertion that reason was the sole certain source of knowledge. It is generally accepted that this evolution in Western thought dates from the time of the Renaissance. But might you not object that the rejection of women is much more ancient than that?

Well, it seems that that is not so. At that time there also occurred a change in the attitude of men towards women, a change of which I too had no suspicion when I began the preparation of this book, and on which the feminist writers whom I was reading were silent. On the contrary, they claimed to be fighting for the liberation of woman from her 'medieval condition', thus allowing it to be understood that before the Renaissance contempt for women was general and unrelieved.

Now, that is not true. In the Middle Ages women were much more highly respected and active in social life. My eyes were opened by a book quoted by Marc Oraison, written by a woman historian, a specialist in the subject, named Régine Pernoud. 'How many of the militants in feminist movements', she writes, 'honestly think that women have always been confined at least in a moral gynaeceum, and that it is only the progress made in our twentieth century which has afforded them some liberty of expression, and more freedom in work and in their personal lives?'

The fact is that in the Middle Ages women could achieve political power. In France queens were crowned with as much solemnity as kings, by the same Archbishop of Rheims. And it was not just a matter of reigning, but also of governing, exercising power, a power much more absolute than that of any politician of our own day. 'An Eleanor of Aquitaine, a Blanche of Castile,' writes Régine Pernoud, 'really dominated their century.' That did not prevent them from having children, since Eleanor had ten, as also did Catherine de Medici.

But it does not apply only to queens. Régine Pernoud writes: 'We find women voting alongside men in city assemblies and in rural communes.' That they did so in complete independence of mind is

19

witnessed to by the case of Gaillardine de Fréchou, who 'was the only one to vote *no,* when all the rest of the population voted *yes'*. Abbesses wielded extraordinary power in the Middle Ages. There was even one double monastery, that is to say including not only a monastery for men but also a convent for women, which was under the authority not of an abbot, but of an abbess – in fact a young woman of twenty-two. 'The nuns of those times were mostly extremely well-educated women who could have competed with the most cultured monks.' Political equality and cultural equality were facts.

What about economic life? – 'In legal deeds it is quite common to find a married woman acting on her own account, opening a shop, for instance, or starting a business, and without being obliged to produce any marital authorization. Finally, the tax registers show large numbers of women in gainful occupations, – schoolmistresses, doctors, apothecaries, plasterers, dyers, scriveners, miniaturists, bookbinders, etc.'

'It was only in the seventeenth century that it became obligatory for women to take their husband's name', a fact which speaks volumes on the root of the problem, the personal autonomy of the woman; as does the fact that 'the conjugal community, the father and the mother, performed conjointly the task of educating and protecting the children and, if required, the administration of their goods'. It will be objected that a daughter was not free to marry whom she chose. True, but in this respect a son was not free either. Equality of the sexes was a fact!

Finally, since we are concerned here with our attitude as men towards women, I cannot conclude this reference without quoting the chapter in Régine Pernoud's book devoted to courtly love, to its wonderfully subtle and delicate songs, so different from ours, and to medieval literature in general, which shows towards women 'a tenderness full of respect'. Eric Fuchs similarly writes: 'With regard to the institution of marriage, courtly love seems to be a claim by the woman to be recognized as such, that is to say, as a person.'

It seems to be the first time in history that the notion of the equality of woman as a person makes its appearance. You will realize that I was profoundly impressed by Régine Pernoud's book. It denounces our prejudices as well as those of the feminists about the condition of women in the Middle Ages. The liberation of women was certainly not complete – nor is it today – but it was more advanced than it had been throughout antiquity.

It was later, therefore, that the brake was applied, and a kind of cultural revolution took place in the relationship between men and women. It happened in the Renaissance, and in the century of French classicism, at the beginning of the modern age. There supervened the great injustice, the forfeiture of their legal rights, the alienation of women.

The injustice was sealed by the rediscovery of Roman law during the Renaissance. Régine Pernoud lays great stress on this point. Medieval law was based on custom and was flexible, varying in a thousand ways from lordship to lordship, in accordance with local franchises and traditions. The adoption of Roman law served the great political movement which followed the Renaissance – the consolidation of royal power, and the urbanization and centralization which was to lead to the modern nation-state. At the same time it sanctioned the lower status of women on the model of ancient Rome. Richelieu himself said, 'Nothing is more capable of damaging the body politic than this sex' (quoted by Benoîte Groult).

This important chronological distinction is confirmed by another historian, Jean Delumeau, of the Collège de France. Régine Pernoud was a specialist in the Middle Ages, and used every effort to clear that period of the false accusations made against it. Jean Delumeau, on the other hand, specializes in the Renaissance, and he too dates from that time the change we are discussing, and he too attributes it to the introduction of Roman law. Furthermore, he explains how this came about.

He shows how we have been misled by what he calls 'the seductive term "Renaissance" '. It is true that because it gave us so many treasures of art, literature, and philosophy, we are only too ready to picture it as a sort of golden age in which men were able to devote themselves in all quietness to the most serene pursuits. The reality is that it was an age of the most terrible fear, anguish and panic. One catastrophe followed hard upon another: the plague, which made a 'shattering reappearance', the Great Schism, famines following disastrous harvests, rebellions everywhere, the ravages of undisciplined soldiery in the Thirty Years War, the menace of the Turks, and then the Protestant secession. It was, as J. Lortz says, 'an end-of-the-world atmosphere'. Both Catholics and Protestants expected it imminently; they delved into the apocalyptic prophecies, and saw Satan everywhere: he it is, 'obviously ... who is waging his last furious war before the end of the world. In this supreme assault

21

he uses every means and every subterfuge. It is he who is behind the Turkish advance; he is the inspiration of the heathen religions of America; he dwells in the hearts of the Jews; he is responsible for perverting the minds of heretics; he it is who, thanks to the feminine wiles of a sex long considered guilty, seeks to seduce from their duty the defenders of public order; he it is who, through sorcerers, and especially through witches, disturbs daily life by casting spells on men, beasts, and crops. One cannot be surprised that these various attacks all come at once.'

You will recognize the mechanism of the scapegoat, well known to psychologists. In extreme adversity people look for somebody to blame and to denounce. The agents of Satan are the Turks, the Jews, heretics (the Protestants or the Papacy, depending on one's point of view), and women. The Turks are powerful enough to look after themselves; Catholics and Protestants likewise have their armies, and will wage terrible wars of religion against each other, all fighting the same enemy – Satan. But the heathens in South America are defenceless against the carnage that will blot out their ancient civilizations. Lastly, neither Jews nor women have any means of defence, and so they will be persecuted.

And so we find the trials of witches, which so many people think of as belonging to the Middle Ages. In fact they only reached their full tragic extent in the Renaissance, and were at their worst in the seventeenth century, in the time of Descartes, whom no one would assign to the Middle Ages! Thus at the very moment when that philosopher was formulating the principles of the scientific rationalism which was to inspire the modern age, the most impressive manifestation of irrational fear of woman was rampant. Is not this due to the fact that she is looked upon by man as a fascinating mystery, connected in some way with the irrational power of the emotions?

Even the famous aphorism, 'I think, therefore I am' of Descartes, and its success, are probably a reaction to the great panic described by Jean Delumeau. He does not say so, but it seems to me that it may well be seen in that light – a search for security in the midst of disorder, for a solid foundation for thought at a time when theologians, the carriers of an irrational message, are floundering in endless controversy.

With his 'I think, therefore I am,' man is on his own, concerned with himself; he stands alone, with no other reference than his 'I', without reference to an 'us', to anyone else, to any relationship with another. That is the source of modern individualism – modern and masculine. It is woman who has a primordial need for relationship. She has no consciousness of existing except through relationship. She would say 'I relate, therefore I am.' For man, relationship comes later, or even perhaps not at all. In the choice made by the Renaissance, relationship was forgotten.

I am not arguing against rationalism. It is legitimate and necessary; it is the masculine principle; what I deplore is the stifling of its non-rational complement, relationship. I was once actually invited by a 'Rationalist Society' in France to give a lecture, and was delighted to do so. The chairman was a colleague of whom I am very fond, and who, rationalist though he is, has a sense of relationship. I was made very welcome. I spoke of this quality of personal relationship which is so rare in our present society. A lively discussion followed, without any trace of philosophical controversy. The real problem is a psychological one: it is that this world of things, however technically advanced, leaves unsatisfied the need for personal relationship which is in every human heart.

Thus there took place at the Renaissance and at the beginning of the modern age a great psychological event: a choice, to the disadvantage of feeling and to the advantage of reason, to the prejudice of the body and the profit of the intellect, at the expense of the person in favour of things. Much more – a kind of repression took place: the repression of affectivity, of sensitivity, of the emotions, of tenderness, of kindness, of respect for others, of personal relationship, of mystical communion – and of woman, with whom all the terms in this list are linked by spontaneous association of ideas. Such is our modern Western world, advanced, powerful, efficient, but cold, hard, and tedious; a world in which diseases accessible to objective study are vanquished, but in which neuroses related to lack of love are multiplied; in which we have amassed a great wealth of things, while the quality of life has deteriorated. The quality of life belongs to a different order, that of feeling.

Feminists are fighting to remove an injustice. I agree with them, but I add that that injustice was an error, the price of which is this civilization of ours that is so lacking in humanity. That error on the part of the Renaissance, and the relegation of women to an inferior status since then, are two aspects of the same problem – the loss of a sense of the person. One can understand why Emmanuel Mounier has spoken of having the Renaissance all over again, but this time making it a rebirth to a sense of the person.

23

However, things have already begun to change. Scientists have given up their claim to be promoting a golden age through technological progress. Many young people are rejecting this impersonal society. And women have begun to attack the palisade, to make breaches in the walls of their prison, and to break out from 'inside'. I borrow this simple, ordinary terminology from Claude Enjeu and Joana Savé. In a symposium entitled *Les femmes s'entêtent* ('Women Insist') they refer to these two territories – 'inside' and 'outside', the closed circle of the family and the open space of society – and to the customs-barrier through which men could go outside, but not women.

This conventional barrier, this obstacle to free passage, also bears a simple, ordinary name which I have been surprised not to find in the feminist indictments: it is 'apartheid'. This form of apartheid was still very powerful when I was a child at the turn of the century. When my wife was attending religious instruction classes – she must have been fifteen or sixteen: I did not know her then, but she has told me so often! – her parents did not allow her to come home alone at six o'clock in the evening; the pastor would go with her as far as a square where my father-in-law awaited her.

A precaution against the white slave-trade? – You are joking! Geneva was no less safe to live in then than it is today. No, it just 'was not respectable'. A few years later, when we were engaged, I took her for a ride astride the luggage-carrier of my little motorbike, and I was the one to be criticized, because that was not respectable. Had it been a boy, no one would have said anything.

This apartheid has been removed in part. Such anecdotes serve to show how far we have come in my lifetime. Many women have crossed the threshold of the door to the world 'outside', towards public life, and liberty. Exceptionally, a few occupy important positions in society. We point to them to salve our consciences.

But in order to be accepted they have to adapt themselves to the masculine world that history has fashioned. So, here is the question I ask myself: if one day this apartheid is really abolished, if women manage to win their full place, and to exercise as much influence as men in our society, will they then be able to heal it of the sickness it suffers from, the lack, the loss of a sense of the person? That is my hope. That is why I am writing this book. Because women have, more than men, a sense of the person.

4

Women have a Sense of the Person

I well remember the day when, suddenly and clearly, I realized that fact. I was in the middle of a long speech to my wife – about divorce, if I remember rightly. I thought I was talking to her, but it was not really a dialogue; rather a monologue in which I was getting carried away by the flow of my own ideas. Nelly was listening to me indulgently. But suddenly she interrupted me to ask, 'But who is it you're talking about?'

Her question stopped me in my tracks, and I replied naïvely, 'I'm not talking about anyone in particular, just about the problem of divorce.' Nevertheless, as I spoke I was aware of the distance that separates 'anyone' from 'anything'. Two worlds, as we have seen. Oh I know the difference can be a subtle one, for there is always 'someone' hidden behind 'something'. And yet at that point our two different ways of approaching the problem met and missed each other like strangers in the street. '*Who* is it you are talking about?' she wanted to know. Women are not so much interested in divorce, as in Jacqueline's divorce, or Joan's, or Betty's. Men get more satisfaction from abstract and impersonal problems, from dialectic and intellectual discussion. They are at ease in the world of things and are often oblivious of persons.

I can see, for instance, that among the crop of feminist books that I have been reading, the ones that struck me as the most sympathetic and feminine were not the most scholarly, the most systematic or the most circumstantial. Despite their manifest excesses, it was those which came from the heart rather than the head, those which arose out of a very personal and even shocking experience that attracted me. Feminists will suspect that I am trying to confine women to the conventional model of a capricious and unpredictable being. It is true that though we men sometimes complain about their capriciousness, we are also quite keen for

25

them to remain so, as a counter-weight to our masculine coldness and objectivity.

What I am saying here, however, has a much deeper meaning for me: in discovering how women have a sense of the person, and prefer the living experience to the abstract idea, I saw at the same time how lacking we men are in this sense of the person. And I understood also why it is that our Western civilization has evolved towards the predominance of things over persons during the last four centuries, in which men by banishing women from the life of the community have deprived themselves of their influence.

When I was leaving home to give a lecture my mind would be entirely occupied by the thought of what I was going to say, and how best to present it in order to be understood and to persuade my audience. My wife, for her part, would be more concerned with brushing my coat collar. I was preoccupied with ideas, she with my person, my personal presentation.

Last year in Tokyo, now a widower, I was hastening among the profusely flowering shrubs in the marvellous gardens of the International University on my way to the chapel, to talk about the crisis in our civilization. I heard hurrying footsteps behind me, and there, brush in hand and anxious to perform the little necessary service for me, was Mrs Shin, the Korean assistant of one of my publishers – a woman!

I begin this chapter with anecdotes which will no doubt strike men who read this as being rather trivial, but in which women will perhaps recognize themselves. At any rate they illustrate the role which my wife has played in my own development. If I have become the leading advocate of the medicine of the person, constantly reminding my colleagues that the patient who consults them is not just a case, but also a person, and that establishing a personal relationship with him contributes to his treatment, it is above all due to the influence of my wife.

Of course I influenced her as well. When I married her she was extremely shy; she did not dare to speak in public, and thought herself incapable of handling intellectual ideas because she had hated school. And then it came. She found that she could hold her own in discussions, and that liberated her from feelings of inferiority towards me. One day she talked to me about the parable of the talents, which had been the subject of her meditation. She told me that it had occurred to her that now she was trying too hard to imitate me and my own particular talents, and that in the evening of her life she would be asked what she had done with her own talents, not mine.

That is why I say today that women have a mission. After three centuries of being thrust aside they are now mostly endeavouring to imitate men, to demonstrate that they are capable of doing any job men can do. That equality is still a long way off, but that they are capable of it has been demonstrated. So perhaps the next stage is that they will determine to make a more personal contribution to our civilization by doing what they can do better than men, using their special talent for attention to persons and not only to things.

In order for this to happen they must first realize that this is their mission. It is in that hope that I am writing this book, at least to invite them to think about it. And also to open men's eyes to expect something more from women than subservient collaboration in masculine activities. Women suffer more than we do from the impersonality of our society. I have been the recipient of enough confidences from them to know that. Instead of suffering from it, they could transform it.

My wife Nelly put this mission into practice before my very eyes, through the often very strong links she forged with many of my patients; and also through accompanying me on all my lecture tours. 'If you are on your own', she used to say, 'it's a speech; if I am with you, it is a personal testimony.' But I think above all of our international sessions on the medicine of the person, known as the Bossey Group. It was the extreme care and interest she showed towards each participant that helped to create the personal atmosphere of those meetings. In any other medical conference only ideas matter, and the delegates are appreciated only in terms of their scientific in-put. But in the Bossey meetings everyone was made welcome and was valued as a person; it made no difference whether they were learned scientists or not, brilliant orators or not, women or men.

Now Nelly is dead, but the spirit subsists. Other women are exerting their influence, and the young colleagues who have taken over from me the direction of the sessions understand this well. They take care to preserve their personal character. Not, of course, that ideas and the exchange of ideas are looked down upon, but ideas are seen in a personal context, and not merely as detached academic theories.

They have even almost entirely abandoned the old tradition of master lectures, so as to be able to devote time to the personal experiences and problems of delegates, as well as to Bible study conceived not as lessons in theology but as the study of our own difficulties in the light of the Bible. It is making the Group into a sort of personalist society. I always remember a letter I had from a Dutch professor after one of our sessions, in which he wrote: 'For the first time in my life I have really understood what is meant by the communion of saints ...'

Of course we ought to ask ourselves whether there are biological factors underlying the predominance in men of an interest in things, whereas women are more interested in persons. This does indeed appear to be the case. It is in fact the sole domain in which a difference may be noted educationally between boys and girls, while in every other respect their aptitudes are remarkably similar. This comes out clearly in several of the essays in a symposium edited by Evelyne Sullerot under the title 'The Feminine Fact', in particular that of René Zazzo on the differential psychology of the sexes.

He notes 'the verbal superiority of girls', and the 'superiority in spatial aptitudes of boys' which favours 'technical aptitudes, already noticeable when schooling begins', which 'may be as much as 50% to 100% greater than those of girls. In regard to the verbal aptitude of girls, which makes them better at languages, 'it is evident well before they learn to read'.

Now, what is it that occupies space? – It is things. The person has no spatial dimension. The tests for spatial aptitude are well known: the subject is required to picture to himself an object, a geometric volume or a more or less complicated machine, and to turn it round mentally in space, to manipulate it, to make various sections of it. Men like objects because they like to manipulate, because they are good at it. They are more ready to manipulate women, both physically and morally, than to seek a person-to-person relationship with them.

What, on the other hand, is this 'verbal aptitude'? It is an interest in interpersonal communication, which leads girls to choose, as Evelyne Sullerot writes, 'jobs which bring them into contact with persons rather than things'. This fully confirms what we suspected, that there are innate dispositions which orientate man towards the world of things and woman towards the world of persons. Small boys already show a preference for mechanical toys, electric trains (on which their fathers are just as keen!), while girls prefer not only

28

dolls, but puppet theatres or toy shops, which give them a chance to serve and chat with imaginary customers.

One of the most interesting differences is in cerebral localizations, which are unilateral, but not always on the same side. Thus the centre of language is usually in the left hemisphere of the brain, but it may be on the right in a left-handed person, who will retain the power of speech despite a cerebral haemorrhage in his left hemisphere. There are more left-handed persons among men than among women; in particular, dyslexia is four or five times more common among boys than among girls. This derives from the fact that 'the degree of specialization of the hemispheres is not the same in the two sexes, lateralization of functions being less common among women', a fact which would facilitate substitution.

The most remarkable thing in all this is that 'it has now been well established that for the great majority of individuals the left hemisphere is predominant in dealing with analytical, linguistic and sequential tasks. The right hemisphere is predominant in dealing with global, non-verbal, and spatial tasks'. That would explain the liking of men for big abstract theories, and that of women for the small concrete details. It would also explain 'the fact that there are so few women architects, engineers, or artists ... [because] these professions require the manner of thinking and of perception of space which is best performed by the right hemisphere'.

So you see: it would appear that we perceive the world of things with our right hemisphere, and the world of persons with our left! It follows that women, whose brains are less lateralized, are less handicapped in the perception of things than are we men in the perception of persons.

There is therefore a singular convergence between what has been borne in upon me by my own experiences, and the results of scientific research – the two poles of knowledge. That is, that men are better fitted for the construction of a world of things, and women a world of persons. They ought therefore, it seems to me, to work more closely together as equal partners, each carrying out his or her own mission, to achieve a more harmonious world.

I could quote other observations in confirmation of these views. Who is it, for example, who remembers people's birthdays? Women, more often than men. It is the wife who will be wondering all day long whether her husband is going to remember that it is their wedding anniversary. It is all right if when he comes home in the evening he brings a bouquet of red roses or some special present. But that does not always happen. Nevertheless she has been arguing with herself all day, telling herself that her husband loves her and that she ought not to measure his love by a little detail of that sort – he has so many other things to think about; and yet she is really put out if he does not remember. Women are better at remembering anniversaries because they pay more attention to the person.

I cannot refrain from mentioning other examples, drawn from present trends in our society. Take ecology: everyone is talking about it nowadays, yet a mere ten years ago the word was used only among a few specialists. Whence comes this sudden explosion, which constitutes an important event, since it indicates a profound change in our conception of the world? It expresses exactly the malaise felt by our excessively technological civilization.

It is the realization that Nature is not just a stock of raw materials which can be drawn on indefinitely and manipulated regardless of any other criterion than the needs of the economy. Also that civilization is made for man, not man for civilization; that what is useful – a masculine criterion – must not be sought at the cost of the destruction of what is pleasant – a feminine criterion.

This was already well understood by a handful of specialists. But their voice was scarcely heard at all by a world that was greedily seeking after things. Certainly it was not loud enough to set going a vast movement of public opinion, so vast that now it is having electoral repercussions, disturbing the equilibrium of the traditional political parties for the first time for centuries. For that, a collective emotion was needed. And is not emotion the peculiar gift of the woman? It was in fact a woman who sensitized and aroused public opinion – Rachel Carson, with her book *Silent Spring*.

Then there were the women in Northern Ireland who were awarded the Nobel Peace Prize for their work in organizing a women's movement against the civil war, at the risk of being looked upon as traitors by both sides. 'This Irish story has proved, better than anything else, the difference between masculine and feminine objectives', writes Michèle Perrein. 'Men kill each other on account of rights and ideas. Women rise up and declare that no one has a right to kill their children.'

Of course, the problem of war is a complex one, and for my part I do not think one can impute it solely to men. But who could deny that the wild wind of desire for power that has been blowing on the

West since the Renaissance, throughout the last three centuries during which men have stopped asking women for their opinion, has not only stimulated their creative genius, but also fanned the flames of their conflicts? Even at school boys are more pugnacious than girls.

Turning to the sphere of medicine, I recall a discussion about the medicine of the person in the hospital, where it is without doubt more difficult to practise than in the consulting room. One of us was making a plea for small hospitals, saying that it was impossible in large ones. Then Professor Richard Siebeck, who was the head of an enormous establishment, intervened: 'I do not think that the question of scale is the most important thing. Our good fortune at Heidelberg is that we have a matron who is so personal herself that everyone who comes into contact with her becomes personal.' I have also been particularly struck by a book by Thérèse Bertherat and Carol Bernstein, entitled 'The Body has its Reasons'. Thérèse Bertherat is a physiotherapist, and the widow of a psychiatrist who was tragically murdered by one of his patients. Her book begins with an account of this incident, and is very personal from beginning to end. She tells of her distress, until the day she met a pupil of Françoise Mézières, the creator of a revolutionary method of gymnastics.

Or rather, as she calls it, 'anti-gymnastics', for she takes an opposite line to the methods conceived by men who, with their mechanical outlook, see the body as a machine, each part of which must be separately manipulated, and who actually devise ingenious machines to impose these manipulations upon it. She writes movingly about a psychotherapy conference at which a particularly sophisticated example of one of these devices was proudly displayed. Thérèse Bertherat was fascinated not by the machine, but by the look of terror in the wide brown eyes of the child who was fastened to this instrument of torture. 'He had good reason to be terrified', she says.

There we have three women – Françoise Mézières, her pupil, and the author of the book – who are bringing to the correction of bodily malformations a real medicine of the person, since its aim is to make the patient aware of his own body, and to reconcile him with it, and to sharpen his sensibility. It seeks physical and moral détente, instead of the reinforcement of muscle, with which men are always obsessed. It is not unlike the method of Dr Roger Vittoz for the treatment of neuroses through control by the brain over the body.

Lastly I should like to mention one more woman, also a doctor, of whom my readers will doubtless have heard, even if they have not read her books, Elizabeth Kübler-Ross. She has taken the lead in promoting dialogue with the dying. She saw that most patients were adandoned to utter loneliness at the approach of death, because no one dared to enter into sincere dialogue with them. What were their feelings in the extreme situation in which they found themselves? No one really knew, because no one gave them a chance to talk about them. And yet they needed to express their feelings now more than ever.

The family, near relatives, and friends, either did not know what to say – at a time when listening was really more important than talking – or else they talked about all sorts of trivial and unrelated matters in order to distract the patient, and to avoid having to talk about what was really on his mind. It is truly tragic when a husband and wife who have been deeply attached to each other, having no secrets from each other, who have often prayed together perhaps, are morally and spiritually separated in this way at that supreme moment. Or perhaps they tell each other pious white lies which deceive neither of them, since very often the patient from whom one is hiding the truth has in fact guessed it.

Elizabeth Kübler-Ross too is personal. She tells of how she realized that it was her own fear of death which was preventing her from entering into dialogue, and that she had to overcome that in order to be ready for it. She describes the death of her father, which took place much later. She had been recalled from America to his bedside in Switzerland because he was dying. And there, specialist as she was in the dialogue with the dying, she found herself beginning to talk about all sorts of things in order to create a diversion – because her emotion was so much greater with her own father.

Finally, after a great inner struggle, she could stand it no longer, and she said, quite simply, 'Why are we talking like this? You know quite well why they sent for me!' And at once the ice was broken, their tongues were loosed, happy memories from the past came crowding in and she was able there and then to have with her father one of the most marvellous conversations of her life.

I have mentioned the family and friends. What about the doctor? It is even more difficult for him. He is more embarrassed than anyone when faced by death. It is very often he who recommends that the truth should be concealed from the patient. He creates a diversion by prescribing yet another X-ray, a laboratory test, or a new drug. Or else he calls less often, or pretends to be in a hurry, because he is afraid of a direct question, and he finds the feeling of his own impotence intolerable.

It is important to see that all I have said about the contrast between scientific objectivity and personal relationship is also involved here. The doctor has had a scientific training at medical school. He is perfectly happy so long as all he is called upon to do is to discuss the case, to make a diagnosis, to prescribe treatment – in short, to do something. Indeed, doing something belongs to the world of things. And when there is nothing more to do, how does he cross over into the world of persons? The famous seminars conducted by Elizabeth Kübler-Ross, which so many of my colleagues attend, are lessons in the medicine of the person given by a woman. That is indeed a woman's mission.

Four years ago Nelly and I were in Athens where I was lecturing. While we were there she suffered a severe coronary thrombosis. For a month she was wonderfully looked after in intensive care, surrounded by our Greek friends. For us that was a time of supreme intimacy, for as we were away from home I was able to give all my time to her. We spent a lot of time in silent communion, a lot of time in prayer, but there was also plenty of time for real dialogue about our feelings.

On the morning of Ascension Day she asked me again whether we were afraid she would suffer a second coronary, and on my reply she said with great emotion, 'In that case I am quite certain I shall die.' But after expressing her fear in those words, she also expressed her hope, and in a concrete manner which touched me greatly: 'If I had died a month ago I should be in heaven now, and I should be meeting your parents.' I replied, very simply, 'When you meet them in heaven they will thank you for having been the wife that you have been for their son.'

It was the last thing I said to her. A few minutes later she put her hand on her heart, and said, 'That's it!'

'Are you sure?'

'Yes.'

And she died. My first thought was that it was a beautiful death.

5

The Fear of Emotion

As we have seen, the great obstacle to personal contact is the fear of emotion. That is true not only in the face of death, but at every moment of life. Everything that is truly personal to us, everything that involves us as persons, raises a wind, if not a storm, of emotion: love, guilt, faith, grief or joy, success or failure, and creativity.

Notice that it is not so much the emotion we are afraid of, as letting it show, revealing ourselves in the heat of emotion, betraying ourselves. Emotion is so bound up with life itself, in animals as well as in man, that it cannot be eliminated. The expression of emotion is repressed in our society – or rather it is suppressed entirely into the unconscious, as I have said, since it is not a question of a deliberate act of the will, but a phenomenon so spontaneous that it is unconscious. As we all know, emotion re-emerges in our dreams. Men, even more than women, must save face in front of others by putting on a mask of impassibility, in accordance with the model of dignity imposed by society.

When we are shielded from the gaze of others, we may give way to emotion. How many people there are who, in the darkness of the cinema, or in the privacy of their armchairs in front of the TV, find a certain relief in shedding secret tears as they watch frightening or sentimental films; or who write poetry which they keep locked away in a drawer; or who paint pictures which they never put on show.

Clandestine emotions, however, are sterile. I would not feel so much emotion as I write these lines were they not to be published. It is not only the fear of criticism, but also the fear of revealing oneself personally. What is more, I am not a real writer; I have no literary pretensions. I write as a doctor, in order to help other people in their lives and their sufferings. But the fact is that the essential thing in helping them is not so much that I write, as that I enter into a certain personal relationship with them, giving of myself – a relationship charged with emotion.

34

That is why I experience such intense emotion as I write, turning my thoughts over and over in my mind and changing ten times the plan of this chapter, instead of taking the plunge and getting on with it. And yet I know well that here, as in my consulting room, I help others only by accepting this emotion, which is a sharing of their own, by taking it upon myself, by experiencing it myself instead of observing it coldly.

This is the case too with real writers, and with artists of every kind. In any creative work the author is always committing himself, unveiling himself; in a way he is offering his personal emotion to another known or unknown person, hoping to enter into accord with him, to share his emotion with him. The fear is that he will fail in this communication, hear no answering echo, meet rejection or indifference.

In general, women are more emotional, while men have great difficulty in expressing their feelings, or even in allowing them to be guessed at. And just because a man finds it hard to express his feelings, he cannot relate, he is embarrassed, disconcerted, unable to respond. He defends himself by laughing at feminine sensibility, or at least by devaluing it as a sign of weakness.

Many women are hurt by this. They blame themselves for being too emotional, when really the ability to show emotion is a wonderful gift. Even Descartes did not hide the fact that his rationalist philosophic system arose out of an instant of intense emotion. And what of Pascal, Kierkegaard, even Marx, and so many other creative thinkers? Emotion is indeed creative: every creative act is always full of emotion.

In reality, those women who consult their doctors because of their emotionalism are not suffering from that so much as from not being able to control it or direct it towards creative tasks. And I think that the mission of women, which I am writing about in this book, involves especially this fruitful use of their sensibility, a sort of sublimation of it.

For lack of finding an opportunity of doing so in our masculine society, women are reduced to anger and frustration. The ones to blame in my view are ourselves, men, who shut emotion out instead of welcoming it. I have often experienced this myself. An emotional outburst by my wife petrified me into silence. Even though I knew my reaction was the very thing that would increase her emotion tenfold, I could not help it.

It was lucky for me that she did not thereupon conclude, like so many other women, that I was a cold, insensitive man. On the contrary, she saw my reaction as proof of my sensitivity. Very subtle, that, but very important! It is the source of many a mis-understanding between husbands and wives. 'I had just lost my mother', cries one of the women questioned by Claude Maillard, 'and was still suffering from the shock of her death. I had a tremendous need for tenderness, but I fell in with the coldest, most undemonstrative man you could possibly dream of.'

Obviously I do not know the case in question, but I can well imagine that it was precisely because his wife had such an over-flowing emotional need that the husband, unable to respond to it, became icy cold. I have seen it happen with so many couples. Many a wife has said to me, 'I don't seem able really to communicate with my husband. I never know what he feels!' If I had talked to the husband about it, he would have protested: 'What? No communication? But we talk about all sorts of things! What more does she want? How difficult women are to understand!'

I cite here examples of married couples, but the problem is more general, and is to be found in relationships between the sexes in social life, in every office, every club, in churches, and in leisure activities. The emotions have always to be hidden, and emotional subjects avoided. Nor is the problem confined to married women; it also affects unmarried women, who suffer just as much from the impersonal character of our society. For them it is made worse because there is one emotional subject which they must conceal more than any other: the desire for marriage. They above all feel that they are treated as things, as work machines, without any regard for them as persons. The subject is made even more difficult by the fact that men, obsessed always by sex, are quick to suspect the unmarried woman of trying to have an affair if she allows her emotional need to show, even if all she asks is a little sympathy for the hard life she so often leads.

The main problem, then, is with men and the great difficulty they have in expressing their feelings. Is it that they are less sensitive than women, as people say? I am not sure. But they hide and repress their emotion, to the point of being unconscious of it. And that is why they are afraid of it in others. Freud's famous censorship comes into play, to prohibit the return of the repressed emotion. Even Socrates sends the women away while he drinks the hemlock, and admonishes Apollodorus for bursting into tears.

It is men, therefore, who are handicapped in this respect,

deprived of one of the most human qualities of their nature, and that is why they are generally so impersonal. We see it clearly in the meetings of the Bossey Group, to which, nevertheless, doctors come precisely in order to learn about personal relationships. To that end we ask them to talk about their own lives, and the experiences which have aroused their emotions most keenly.

Newcomers to the meetings are aware of this, and are afraid in advance. I find one of them in his room, perplexed and anxious, in front of a blank sheet of paper. He is an eminent scientist, quite ready to deliver a brilliant lecture, but he tells me, 'I have nothing interesting to say about my personal life.'

Men are often affected by this sort of paralysis in the expression of their feelings. Alcohol or sexual desire can take the brake off, but only temporarily. So that during courtship or on the honeymoon a man may become personal and even volubly so. He talks and talks in words full of warmth and poetry, and his partner is dazzled! But the day soon comes when he can no longer talk in any but an impersonal fashion.

That is why his wife is always asking him, 'Do you love me?' Often his only reply is a gesture of irritation, or else he hedges: 'You know very well.' Yes, she knows, but she would like to hear him tell her. At best, the husband drops in at the florist's on his way home, having seen the notice 'Say it with flowers'. She thanks him for the flowers, but dare not tell him she would have preferred him to say it another way.

Upbringing is partly to blame. 'Remember,' writes Marabel Morgan, 'that he grew up in a culture that taught him not to cry when he scratched his leg.' 'You are a boy,' he was told; 'only girls cry.' And in this way he was taught both to despise women, and to look upon the most natural expression of feeling as unworthy of a man. This training is particularly marked in aristocratic and upper middle-class families, to the point of real inhumanity. Many women have said to me, 'I have never seen my husband weep ...'; but they were the ones who were consulting me, not their husbands!

Nevertheless, it seems to me that upbringing and social suggestion do not suffice to explain the phenomenon. It is too general and too difficult to correct. There is in the man an innate tendency towards repression of the feelings. Just as he is at ease among intellectual abstractions, so he is ill at ease in personal relationships.

I am myself no exception. Only I know how hard I find it to

establish a personal relationship. I am supposed to be good at it, but the opposite is the truth. When I say how shy I am, nobody will believe me. When I am asked how to set about it, I do not know; simply because there is no technique for it. I find it extremely difficult to speak personally. For example, I have just noticed that even in my own inner thoughts I say 'Mother' rather than 'Mummy', and 'Father' rather than 'Daddy'. I am sure that this is not because I lost them both while still a child, but because the former term is objective, and the latter personal; the first denotes a role, the second a relationship.

With a patient one starts, of course, with a technical approach. The doctor's first duty must still be his scientific task. That is quite convenient, since technology often provides a means of entry. For example, the analysis of a dream will remind me of an emotional experience which I have had, or through which I am still passing. If I talk about it the personal relationship will spring into being quite naturally, without premeditation.

But I do not see only the sick. An American lady, Grace Halsell, is planning to visit Europe, and announces that she is coming to see me. She is a writer; I have read one of her books, and have admired her wonderful sensitivity. If she wants to see me it is certainly because she expects this warm personal contact; and that is what frightens me and freezes me already. She is going to be terribly disappointed. I regret having written the books in which I described the emotional solitude from which our world suffers. It is, after all, only by a miracle that I have been able to escape myself, and the miracle would need to be renewed every time – but you cannot manufacture miracles.

What am I to do? I have an idea: I shall reserve a table in a good restaurant. Ah, that's the thing for contact. And then I have decided to confess to her straight away how nervous I have been feeling at the prospect of her visit, how tongue-tied I am when I try to express my feelings. Even if she does not understand me it will be the only way for me to overcome my inner panic.

A man, then, finds it much harder than a woman to let his heart speak. He is much more at ease in the world of objects than in that of persons. Now, this throws a new light on the problem that has been occupying us from the beginning of this book: a man is more comfortable in the world of objects because there he is shielded from the sensibilities and the emotional demands of women, to which he does not know how to respond; shielded also from the fundamental irrational questions raised by life, its mystery and its suffering. This is reminiscent of the 'diversion' of which Pascal wrote. It is perhaps for this reason that Annie Leclerc, addressing men, is able to write, 'Your idea of happiness is always that of diversion.'

There is no doubt that our impersonal civilization has been built by men not only because of their interest in objects and the manipulation of them, but also in order to avoid the embarrassing situations which personal relationship involves. It is an escape. The remark was made to me only the other day by Pastor Alain Blancy of the Bossey Ecumenical Institute. I had been talking on this subject before an exciting audience which comprised twenty-eight different nationalities; and those by whom I was most impressed in the discussion which followed were a black from South Africa, an Ethiopian of imposing presence, and a young woman from Fiji. Indeed, other cultures have preserved greater emotional warmth and a keener sense of community, and those who come from such backgrounds are better able than are we who are immersed in it to see how our own culture is lacking in these qualities.

Our own society is anonymous and functional. Each of its members is defined not as a person, but by his role, by the function he performs. It matters little who he is and what are his personal problems. All that is demanded of him is that he fulfils his function; his intimate feelings do not count. The principle is openly stated: 'Business is business'; which means that feelings do not come into it; nor do scruples of conscience. One's relationships with others are only functional. And it works: it is possible for people to work effectively together for years without ever really getting to know each other, without putting an indiscreet question, knowing nothing whatever about each other's essential preoccupations.

It works like a machine all of whose parts are interchangeable. Men have an innate mechanical bent. Even when doing things about the house a man usually prefers the more technical tasks. His wife could probably mend the blown fuse herself, but she allows him the pleasure of doing it. Our masculine society turns like an enormous machine, inexorably. In such a world a woman is handicapped. My father-in-law always used to say, 'Women and machines don't use the same door.' Obviously, that did not encourage his daughter's interest in mechanical things. But a woman can be embarrassing with her emotional preferences: 'I like this, I hate that.' – Why? – 'I don't know, but that's the way it is.' End of argument.

Among men, on the other hand, the possibilities of arguments are endless, because the only things that are discussed are technical problems. Men love looking for new syntheses and clever solutions. But syntheses work only in the world of objects, never in personal relationships. And of course one of the joys of machinery is that you can combine various pieces endlessly one with another, so as to make even bigger and more complicated machines, like the boy with his Meccano set.

This preference for the mechanical seems to me to lie behind three of the great tendencies of our times: first, the centralization of the great nation-states, which contrasts with the patchwork of small communities on the human scale which characterized the Middle Ages. Secondly the concentration of economic power, the growth of trusts and multinationals, in which responsibility is dissipated. Lastly bureaucracy, the plague of our time, as much in the Communist countries as in the West. There too personal responsibility vanishes away. Procedures and rules are multiplied in order to avoid the need for personal judgment. What is right is what conforms with the rule, and the rule is anonymous.

Such is the world which men have constructed in the three or four centuries during which women have been pushed to one side. 'What about nineteenth-century Romanticism?' you will ask me. Listen to the specialists: Certainly, Perrot tells us, the Romantic period was 'a notable liberation of feeling, of the right to weep, to swoon, to bring out into the open all that is kept back nowadays – sentimentality, sensitivity ... Women rushed to take up the new ideology only to find themselves its prisoners.' Aron goes further: 'The fact is that the nineteenth century had a horror of Romanticism.'

What does that mean? Well, it means that it was essentially the century of realism, positivism, industrialization, and the triumph of the world of things, over which reason, objectivity, and profit reigned. Obviously the emotions – and women – could not be abolished, and so they were relegated to the wings, kept behind the scenes. There women could swoon, and Victor Hugo could sentimentalize about the poor without disturbing the action on stage. Neither Romanticism nor women influenced the course of history. Where, then, were women 'imprisoned', to use Perrot's term? Precisely off-stage, exiled from the reality of life. It is of this exile that I am talking here.

This image of the stage and the wings appeals to me. I have spoken of the repression of the emotions into the unconscious. The unconscious, as depth psychologists have revealed to us, is as it were the wings of our personal lives, a back-stage area where strings are pulled to manipulate the scenery, and where the prompter stands whispering to the actor the lines he is to recite.

The world of things has been a wonderful adventure for men, in love as they are with technology, power, and efficiency. But women are the sufferers. Listen to Annie Leclerc: 'The things that men are interested in are not just stupid, fraudulent, and oppressive. Most of all they are dreary, dreary enough to drive one to boredom and despair.' She is joined in this thought by a man, a man sensitive to spiritual values, namely Paul Ricoeur, who has spoken of the boredom of highly industrialized societies.

Let us be fair: Annie Leclerc says elsewhere, 'I think that women are capable of acting just as badly and just as stupidly – why not? But let us not forget that this society was not made by them, and it is manifestly bad for them.' Have we not forgotten the complementarity implicit in the nature of man and woman, and God's own intention when he says that it is not good for man to be alone (Gen. 2.18)? Would it not be better for both to act together, rather than one on the stage and the other in the wings?

Women are now beginning to come back on-stage. It has not yet made much difference, it seems to me. This may be because they have had to start by playing the game as it is, and conform to the masculine model. In politics, for instance, they have docilely slipped into the age-old mould of the traditional parties. But if women dared to be themselves, to realize their special mission, and if their influence increased, would our society become more humane?

41

6

Women at Home and at Work

In a bookshop, in order to get some idea about a new book I have noticed, I generally go straight to the table of contents. I imagine that if some feminist or anti-feminist – woman or man – does that with this book, he or she will light upon the title of this chapter and open the book at this page. He will be trying in this way to put an instant label on me: am I for or against Women's Lib., for or against careers for married women?

Not having read my earlier chapters, he will be disappointed, and even irritated, that I do not take sides. He will not understand that when I say that I believe women have a mission my purpose is not to dictate to women what they should do, but to help them to see for themselves what with their sensitivity and their sense of the person they can contribute to society wherever they are – in the home, at work, or in politics. The mission of which I speak concerns all women, including the unmarried who are indeed obliged to work, especially if they stay at home looking after aged parents.

For me to try and lay down the law about the personal choices open to women would be quite ridiculous, since I am a man. Above all it would be to treat them as not fully responsible, to deny their liberty and my own training as a psychotherapist – it is well known that the latter is careful not to set himself up as a director of conscience; that his aim is to see the person consulting him becoming aware of his own convictions; that in order to do so he must himself give as little directive as possible, and be as free as possible from every kind of prejudice, since it is the prejudices of his patient's parents in his childhood, and now those of his social environment, which are blocking his personal development.

Quite the opposite is the case with most of the books I read on this subject. I find a cross-fire of declarations of principle and contradictory advice. This mode of abstract and theoretical argument is more masculine than feminine, and I am surprised to find it coming from the pens of women. There are, of course, plenty of valid arguments, both in favour of the married woman devoting herself to the home and in favour of her taking up a career. In such arguments, as in marital conflicts, each side is right and can easily demonstrate the fact provided care is taken to underline what the other does not see, and not to see what the other underlines.

France Quéré shows how sterile is this theoretical controversy about the woman's role; a controversy which, she tells us, has distant origins: it goes right back to the two biblical versions of creation. The so-called Priestly account refers to the simultaneous creation of man and women, of the human race: 'God created man in the image of himself, in the image of God he created him, male and female he created them' (Gen. 1.27). In the Yahwist account it is only later that God decides that it is not good for man to be alone. From one of his ribs he fashions woman and brings her to him for his free acceptance, as 'a helpmate suitable ... for him' (Gen. 2.18-23).

From then on throughout history two camps confront each other: one sees the similarities between man and woman, their equality and their indissoluble solidarity; the other stresses their differences, the subordination of woman, and her distinct purpose. The argument is unending, because neither side is trying to understand the other, but only to argue. Each camp has made up its mind, and on occasions is not averse to fudging the evidence. Betty Friedan, who maintains, as we shall see, that a woman cannot develop fully if she stays at home, tells amusingly of how a certain psychoanalyst protested to her that he knew four such who were quite fulfilled. She went and checked each one: all were in fact career women.

Worst of all is the practice of setting women against each other: 'It is absurd,' writes Jacqueline Gelly, 'to set up an artificial barrier between women at work and women at home.' And Le Garrec: 'The ideal would be for the barriers to come down, and for women at home and career women no longer to see one another as adversaries and rivals.' There are women who give up the chance of marriage in order to take religious vows, some who do so in favour of a career, others who abandon their studies and the prospect of a career in order to marry and have children, and yet others who seek to combine both activities, which is not easy; and those who have not been able to choose, for lack of the opportunity of a satisfactory marriage, might well have preferred to marry and have a family.

As a practitioner I am fully aware of the extreme complexity of the problems facing women, and desire above all things to help every woman to take charge of her own life instead of merely putting up with it. As a psychologist I want to help women to see to what they are committing themselves by the choices they make. One point, for instance, is firmly established, especially since the work done by Spitz: the need of the child for his mother during the first year of life. His mental health during the whole of the rest of his life can depend on it.

In the human race, and in it alone, every child is born prematurely. Among all other mammals the young can move about and seek their own food as soon as they come into the world. Human young reach that stage of development only towards the end of their first year. Because of the slow rate of his biological development, the human child is unable to spend this time of growth still in his mother's womb, and the deficiency can be made up only by the instinctive care of the mother. There is the added factor that in the human species more than any other, the problems of relationship play an essential role in mental development.

And not only in mental, but in personal development as well. The person is not to be equated with the psyche: the body is even more integral to it. That is why the medicine of the person is as interesting to surgeons as it is to psychiatrists. We say that we have seen someone 'in person' or 'in the flesh', and they mean the same thing. The child who in the first months ought still to be in his mother's womb would still be enjoying absolute personal contact with her, since he would be an integral part of her. We can understand therefore why Dr Janov insists ceaselessly on the importance of body to body contact between the baby and his mother, and how vital it is that she should caress him, kiss him, and hold him in her arms. Through his 'primal scream' treatment, rather than through psychoanalysis, his patients are able to recall the memory of extremely early experiences, and in particular the suffering caused by an unsatisfied need for body contact.

This is so important that the law ought to ensure that every young working mother has a year's paid leave, with the right to return to her job thereafter. I am afraid that women themselves would not support such a proposal, for fear of having even more difficulty in finding work. Already in the present situation the only way a girl could have an equal chance of employment, according to Christiane Collange, would be if she could produce 'a medical certificate attesting her sterility'. The cost could, however, be borne by the community, as in the case of retirement pensions.

But children still need their mother on beyond their first year, although then the need is less absolute. Women know this too well for me to have to tell them. Hence the dramatic nature of the inner crisis when they are faced with the choice of sacrificing studies or an interesting career to their longing to have a child. They feel it much more acutely still when the child is there, with his smile, and the wonderful joy in his eyes when his long-awaited mother comes and takes him up in her arms.

Furthermore, before criticizing the woman who has not wanted, or been able, to give up her outside work, we should look at all the sacrifices she is imposing upon herself, the permanent overwork, the tragically hard life she so often has to lead. She may well have to go straight from the office to the supermarket and then be doing housework late into the night when children and husband are asleep.

There is also the problem of latch-key children, the seriousness of which has been stressed by psychiatrists. Many teachers are worried by the child who comes to school with the front door key tied round his neck in case he loses it, because there is no one there to let him in when he gets home from school. 'So let us bless non-working women. Where should we be without them?' writes Christiane Collange, herself a brilliant career journalist, bearing witness to an invaluable solidarity among women which is more widespread than we imagine.

The woman who has given up everything in order to stay at home may perhaps look after a neighbour's sick child; or simply give a welcome along with her own children to a schoolmate whose mother is at work, so that he can at once tell someone what he has been doing during the day at school, for him a long day filled with all sorts of happenings. Then he can learn to express his reactions rather than learning to bottle them up inside himself.

Families are much smaller these days, however. Not so long ago there were still plenty of families with eight or ten children. Now, in the West, there are rarely more than two. Those who fiercely condemn married women going out to work seem to me to be missing the importance of such a great change. Obviously in the past a mother's time was completely taken up by her maternal role, with her numerous offspring, each of which she nursed at her breast for two or three years – to say nothing of all the preserving and jam making she did. To say nothing either of the fact that no sooner was she done mothering her own children than there were grand-children, in still greater numbers, for her to care for.

All that has changed, and it has left a great void. 'The modern woman of western and northern Europe matures earlier,' writes Evelyne Sullerot; 'she marries earlier, has her children earlier, and stops having children earlier than has been the tradition over a long period.' One understands why she worries in advance about this premature void. Rapid developments in both demography and habits are upsetting all predictions. It is not yet possible to tell whether the effects of these two factors will be cumulative, or whether they will cancel each other out.

There is one measure which I think could bring about a consider-able improvement. Basically almost all mothers would like to find some way of reconciling their role in the home with a career or with a more active social life. This reconciliation would be much easier to achieve if it were generally accepted that a married woman should work half-time. A movement in this direction has already begun: according to Christiane Collange, in France 15% of women's jobs are part-time, while in Denmark and Great Britain the proportion is as much as 40%.

I have long been aware, however, that this movement meets with traditional opposition. When I was in practice I often thought that a patient's convalescence would be shortened if he were able to return to full employment gradually. But I also often found that employers were opposed to the suggestion: 'We do not know what to do with a part-time worker: he is never responsible for his work. Let's wait until he has quite recovered, and then we shall be able to rely on him.' The interest of the firm took precedence over that of the person. There would doubtless be some areas in which half-time work would not be feasible, but given good will I think they would be very few. In hospitals, patients accommodate themselves without much difficulty to frequent changes of nurse.

Women are already handicapped by absenteeism. A child only needs to be unwell, and the mother has to stay away from work. Esther Vilar notes: 'Since everyone knows that a woman is only a temporary worker, she is entrusted only with the less important customers.' She therefore suggests a radical reform: half-time work for all, both men and women, five hours a day, five days a week. In this way the married couple would enjoy a full salary, each earning half of it, and each would have half the day alternately to look after the children, who would thus never have to be left alone. An added advantage would be the abolition of the midday break and a corresponding reduction in time lost in travelling. Esther Vilar is a doctor, but she is also a woman with a sense of the person. At any rate she understands the personal needs of children, and believes in true equality in the responsibilities of men and women. Utopian? Could it be that it is we men who are lacking in imagination? As we were saying just now, women are taking their place on the stage once again; and it is in the sphere of employment that this come-back is being most effective so far. But they have had to adapt themselves to a masculine organization of work, conceived by men for men – full-time, leaving their wives at home: 'So you want to work with us? Then you will have to do as we do, conform to our system of work; it is all or nothing.' Perhaps all this will have to be reconsidered, with the emancipation of women.

The masculine organization of work has involved industrializa-tion, because of the preference of men for mechanization, to which I have referred. Remember – it was in the textile industry, in England, that industrialization began. What a wonderful adventure it was for the engineers who constructed the first automatic looms! But for the women, and the men too, who mind and serve these machines it is no longer an exciting adventure at all. It is nothing but a deadening routine. Is not one of the gravest problems of our civilization the formidable disproportion between the handful of people who are interested and excited by their work, and the countless mass of those who hate it, who put up with it only because of the wages it earns them, and for whom life begins only when work ends?

Textiles have in fact been one of the typical areas of female production for thousands of years. Real production: if there had been professional economists during that time they would certainly have counted it in their Gross National Product. Peter Laslett points this out, and adds other products, 'articles of straw, basketry, and lace'. He writes, 'This manufacturing activity was so important that in two English communities at the end of the eighteenth century the work-load of women was higher than it is today, if work in the home is included.'

And the point is that all this production was carried on in their homes by women singing happily and rocking their babies as they worked. The distaff, the spinning-wheel, home weaving, all symbol-ize to us the idea of the happy, active woman. Our old legends always picture Queen Bertha of Burgundy visiting her good people

47

on horseback, her distaff in her hand. You must admit that the materials and costumes of the Middle Ages were finer than those of today. Industrialization, which has enriched the entrepreneur, has deprived women of their age-old productive activity by separating the place of work from the family home.

The first lecture I gave on this theme of the mission of women in the world was deliverd to an audience of four hundred farmers' wives. They themselves had chosen the subject. Never before had I spoken to an exclusively agricultural audience such as this. In order to win their approval I started by telling them that I knew how to milk cows. But then I pointed out that they had the rare privilege in this day and age of working at home with their families.

In other days that was the case more often than not. For the shoemaker, the clock-maker, or the grocer, work and family were all one. The house and the workshop were behind the shop, and all day long they were moving from one to the other. Husband and wife took over from each other and helped each other, now in one place, now in the other. Each could observe and appreciate the work of the other. And it was not unusual for the children home from school to come into the shop to weigh rice or serve the customers.

Of course the working day was longer, but one did not notice that because time spent at work and time spent with the family were all one, whereas today time devoted to the one is taken from the other. The wife was able to gossip with every customer, with one about her drunkard of a husband, with another about her sick daughter, or her son who was having difficulties at school. On Sunday afternoons, between games of cards, husband and wife would work, together still, preparing orders or doing the accounts of their little business.

The wife would know as well as the husband what they were earning, and he would know how much was being spent on the housekeeping. There were conflicts too, certainly, but there was plenty of personal contact. Nowadays, however, husband and wife may even work in the same supermarket without exchanging a single word or even seeing each other, because the husband is in the store while the wife sits in front of an electronic cash register at the check-out. Curious, is it not, that the check-out is usually assigned to women, who are not so keen as men on figures and electronics?

There are still country doctors who enjoy the benefit of being in a husband and wife team. The wife knows all her husband's patients in the village and the surrounding countryside, even in some isolated farm where she has had to go in person to bring him an urgent call because there is no telephone. She issues medicines, does injections, gives valuable advice, adding, 'I'll talk to my husband about it again.' She pauses at the door of the bar with a friendly word of warning for the drinker; at the grocer's she reminds a diabetic of the diet he must follow. She goes in the car to fetch an aged patient to the surgery.

Above all she guesses the secret problems that hide behind the mask of disease, and draws the doctor's attention: 'You ought to have another word with that one; he needs to talk about his life and not only about his ailment.' The doctor's reputation for understanding is due in part to his wife. He may be a first-class technician, but she helps him to see that side of medicine which goes beyond technique, and their life together is enriched by this mutual interchange.

I have also come across restaurants run by real man and wife teams of that kind. But apart from a few privileged occupations, it is rare nowadays to find this community of work anywhere except among the peasant farmers. Even there the numbers are rapidly dwindling under the pressure of mechanization. I remember the haymaking and the harvests of my childhood, with large numbers of happy men and women working with sickle and scythe, hay-fork and rake. Today there is only a solitary man on his tractor, giving free rein to his innate liking for the mechanical. Or else he hires a specialist contractor with some monstrous, noisy, complicated machine.

The mechanization of production is everywhere banishing personal contact. I know well that we can no longer do without machines and all the benefits they have brought us. I am truly masculine in that. All I am saying is that without the counterweight of women and their feeling for personal relationships, men go on blindly increasing production in a way that is pointless if there is no delight in it. Look at the boy with his Meccano set: he builds a crane and is delighted to do it. But after it is made, and he has made it work a few times, he tires of it. He dismantles it in order to construct something new. Men constantly and feverishly do just that.

The little girl, on the other hand, will play happily for hours with her toy grocery shop, because she turns it into a living world. She peoples her world with individuals and identifies with each one; she imagines the story of their lives, their joys and sorrows, and their endless conversations. She enjoys the interchange of feelings. Enjoyment. I come across the word again and again in these books

49

that women write about their problems. For a man, production is measured in the quantity of things produced, but for a woman, in the enjoyment of their use.

7

The Status of Women

I have just been talking about textiles. It is not the only sphere in which women have been deprived of the opportunity of producing something of real economic value while at the same time deriving personal enjoyment from it. My maternal grandmother was the typical active woman of the turn of the century. She was busy in the house from morn till eve. I remember the days when she melted butter: we would look forward gleefully to tasting the candy. And the smell when she was roasting coffee. And then the salting of the various kinds of meat was an art in itself. And the big whole cheese that she ordered every year from Gruyères itself, which she used to keep in a stone vat, wrapped in a cloth soaked in white wine to keep it fresh.

She kept a register of all her guests, with a note of the menu served on each occasion, so as to avoid serving any of them with the same dish twice. To the pastor, who was a total abstainer, she used to offer a home-made liqueur which she called raspberry syrup, and which he greatly appreciated. I remember the fruit picking in the garden, and all the preserves and jams she made. Jam making was a topic of conversation among all the housewives of the district, each having her own special recipe. It is quicker to get it from the supermarket, but nothing like so enjoyable.

Madame Bernheim's irony is all very well: 'The great philosophers are men. The great peelers of potatoes are women.' The remark is amusing, but perhaps its author does not know how many confidences women can exchange in the intimacy of peeling potatoes together. Of course my grandmother employed servants to perform such tasks, but they were part of the family and shared its joys. They became very attached to the children, often having more to do with them than their mother, and the children returned their affection in equal measure.

This was the case with Nelly. Every year I took her to a little village in the canton of Vaud to visit, while she was still alive, an old lady who had played a very important part in her childhood. I too went back to another village to see the woman who had looked after me when my mother was so ill. I realize that domestic servants are a thing of the past; but are many of the monotonous jobs that so many women do in factories really more interesting than peeling potatoes? They are better paid, but they leave the need for personal contact unsatisfied. The clatter of machinery is not conducive to conversation – the secrets of the heart are not to be shouted at the top of one's voice.

In any case, not all husbands are great philosophers. Many intellectuals are surprisingly embarrassed by the problems of every-day life. It may happen that an intellectual loses his wife. She, having had no intellectual pretensions herself, found a meaning for her life, and took pride in being able to minister to her husband's everyday needs, so that he could devote himself to his important work for humanity. She would be told nowadays (in the words of the writer Anaïs Nin) that she lived only by proxy through her husband. But might not one also say of the husband that with regard to material life he lived only by proxy through his wife?

Mention of potatoes reminds me of an anecdote. When Nelly and I were in Germany at a conference of doctors in the spring of 1946, almost the only thing to eat was potatoes in their jackets. We delighted all the participants by bringing coffee and chocolates from Switzerland. At table Nelly became aware that the wife of one of the professors of medicine was staring at her, and she asked her why. 'Don't you peel your husband's potatoes for him?' was the reply. Nelly burst out laughing. 'You don't know him', she exclaimed. 'He is much too independent to allow that!'

At that time there still existed in Germany a veritable veneration for professors! But in venerating their husbands, are not many women also venerating themselves a little? And is it not a little out of jealousy that other women say that they live only by proxy through their husbands? I am no great philosopher, but the problem exists for every couple, and Nelly and I often talked about it. She was so devoted to me that I often wondered whether I was fulfilling her life or stifling it. She was the only one who could provide an answer to that, for it depends not so much on the facts as on what the wife feels.

If there is real dialogue between them, the wife can come to understand and be able to express what she feels, to say whether she feels she does have a personal life of her own, or is living only by proxy. I am astonished when I read these complaints by women that they have only been living by proxy through their husbands, to find no mention of their having talked frankly with their husbands about it. Does not the real problem lie in that lack of dialogue?

It seems to me that a woman is never happier than when she is devoting herself to a man; not only in marriage, but, for example, as secretary to some chief whom she admires and esteems. That men have frequently exploited this natural devotion on the part of women is obvious and outrageous. But, with all 'masculine' objectivity, I have to say that women appear to me to seek this exploitation, or at least to lend themselves too willingly to it, without realizing the fact. My wife often said to me, 'The irritating thing about you is that you are always wanting to manage on your own; one never knows what to do for you.'

Lots of other women have asked me what they could do for me! Certainly it has been in order to please me, but also for the pleasure of pleasing me, a pleasure of which I have deprived them by my proud claim to be able to manage on my own, and my wish not to be beholden to anyone. So I doubt if the feminists will succeed in eradicating from the hearts of women this need to serve. If they devote themselves less to their husbands they will devote themselves more to other men; because it comes from their sense of the person. Whether it be in an office or peeling potatoes, a woman never works for *something*, but always for *someone*. A woman will lose interest in her work and feel herself to be an exploited servant only if she discovers her husband or her employer to be a vain and egotistical person.

I have often peeled potatoes, much more often in the past than now, when as a widower I am happy to buy them ready-peeled in a tin at the supermarket. I recall my pleasure on coming across an ingenious little mechanical potato-peeler. It was just the thing for me, with my masculine interest in machines; but my wife preferred her old potato-knife.

Nelly had no professional career. She belonged to the generation of young women who were beginning to look to something other than artistic accomplishments while awaiting marriage. They were turning rather to some kind of social service than to a job. Influenced to some extent by an older sister, she had begun a course of study at the Institut des Ministères Féminins, which aimed at training women for parish work and giving them some grounding in theology. The course was, however, entirely theoretical, and while it had suited the brilliantly intellectual elder sister, it was quite unsuited to the younger, who had hated school.

She had had to give it up, to her great disappointment. She had had no inkling then that one day she would exercise a real spiritual ministry, founded not upon studies and a diploma, but upon her own personal religious experiences to which she could herself bear witness. This idea, repeated by so many feminists, that it is only academic study, a career, and qualifications that can establish the value of a woman, is an entirely masculine one! The feminists seem at this point strangely influenced by masculine prejudices.

It is part and parcel of the 'functional' society of which I have spoken, conceived by men, in which it is the function that validates the person, and not the person that validates the function.

Those who give way to it are really doubting their own value as persons. Let me make it clear that I am not against women having outside work to the extent that it is compatible with their maternal aspirations. What concerns me is the motivation, that it should be in order to serve the community, rather than to validate themselves.

Let us return now to our historical survey. Men's industrialized society – from which, it is conceded, women also derive some advantages – has deprived women of many of the activities which they undoubtedly enjoyed, and which gave them a certain status because they required skill, and also because in performing them women were their own mistresses, working in their own time, and especially in their own homes alongside their children, or in the homes in which they lived, and without spending hours on tiresome journeys by always inadequate public transport.

This same industrialized society has used women mostly in subordinate, monotonous, and impersonal tasks. It is true that they earn more money for themselves, but their wage depends on the level of the job, let us not forget. That is why in France 'women's earnings are less than 33% of those of men', according to Jacqueline Gelly; and in the USA, according to Kate Millett, the average wages of women represent only half those enjoyed by men.

Mme Francève has made a study of the distribution of jobs in a supermarket. Women made up 90% of the non-supervisory staff, and only 25% of the (much less numerous) supervisory staff. She comments: 'What are they trying to make us believe with the phoney slogan "Equal pay for equal work", when the real question is one of status?' That is indeed the problem. The sociologist

Evelyne Sullerot notes also that women generally occupy subordinate positions, and that promotion for them is slower and rarer. The main argument in favour of work for married women is that it gives them status. All the more reason for not giving the majority of them unimportant jobs.

I do not have to go on quoting statistics. They are available in books, and the evidence is plain for everyone to see in any administrative structure, in industry, commerce, and the arts. I have lectured on the problems of retirement to personnel managers in Lausanne and Geneva. If there is a job for which women are particularly qualified, that must be it! However, there was only one woman among all those gentlemen – and she was the one who had alerted her colleagues to the problems they were discussing.

That is not to say that the said gentlemen have no sense of the person. On the contrary, I must go out of my way to pay homage to their concern. I have worked closely with many of them in pre-retirement seminars, many have become my friends, and I have always admired the spirit of humanity which animates them. It is quite clear that men can take an interest in the person and seek to understand it, as I do myself, in the same way as women today are adapting to jobs that were once the preserve of men. But there it is – the post of personnel manager is an important one in the management structure of an enterprise, and the competition – among men – to climb the ladder is fierce. Among the ranks of company chairmen women are rarer still.

Is the old prejudice still alive, that men are better at giving orders than women? True, men are more aggressive. But I do not think that aggressiveness is the most important quality for becoming a good leader. Women can also rule, but in a different way – from the heart, rather than by raising the voice. You can see this in lots of families in which no one would dream of doing anything of which Mother did not approve. Even a little girl can twist everyone round her little finger. And if the world of business could become a little less aggressive and cruel, do you not think that that would improve the quality of life?

It is a well-known fact that women have fewer fatal car and motorcycle accidents. Men are always tempted to be over bold and to take risks, for the pleasure it gives them when they succeed, which they usually do, though the crash is sudden and catastrophic when it comes. It is no different in politics and business, where men are in command. Our whole society is conceived as a perpetual test of strength: in international relationships, internally between the parties of left and right, and even in the lottery of the court of law, in the confrontation of two eloquent advocates, both equally forceful, tendentious, and unjust.

The same is true of economic and social relationships, between the North and the South, and in labour relations. A lot is said about dialogue nowadays. But men are less gifted in this respect than women. They generally confuse it with argument. The aim of argument, even in formal debate, is to defeat one's opponent. True dialogue seeks to understand him. Solutions are found only when both sides feel they are being understood. Anything else is only a pause while awaiting the opportunity of revenge.

Men are objective, and objectivity always analyses and separates. It is subjectivity which leads to synthesis and union. Obscurely underlying all our conflicts, including the arguments between the generations and between men and women, there is a powerful subjective need on the part of the individual to feel that he is understood, the fulfilment of which is denied in a society that is so poor in personal relationships. An unexpected détente takes place as soon as one of the parties to an argument senses that the other really wants to understand him. And in its turn this détente awakens in him a corresponding desire to understand the other.

Industrial negotiators, whether representing employers or unions, are almost all men; no doubt because their organizations rely on their aggressiveness rather than on their ability to understand others. However, in my country of Switzerland two courageous men, no doubt endowed with a less repressed *anima* than others, have for more than a quarter of a century been personally committed, as representatives respectively of employers and workers, to the search for mutual contact and understanding.

They have succeeded against all expectations and despite general scepticism. The result has been the 'industrial peace' which we still enjoy, imperfect though it is, and which is certainly a major asset in face of the stresses and strains of the present economic crisis. It has brought us more social progress than a free-for-all would have done, despite the very conservative character of our people who, as supreme arbiters in legislative matters, more often than not reject the innovations that are put to them. In passing, I would suggest that that is why my country was the last to accept women's suffrage, because it was the only country in which the decision depended on the people and not on parliament.

But what is the position as regards understanding between men and women? It seems to me that if men understood women better they would expect more of them, and if they expected more of them they would promote them to positions of greater responsibility. Up to now the so-called emancipation of women has meant little, as regards employment, other than allowing them to enter professions formerly reserved for men, provided that they are kind enough to do so in accordance with the rules laid down by men, and that they occupy posts in which they obey orders rather than giving them.

It seems, in a way, as if women have taken up hitch-hiking; men have been willing to let them get into their cars, but have taken good care not to let them do the driving, or even to share it. They do not even like their women passengers to give them advice on how to drive. So the economy remains subject to masculine criteria of rationality, profitability, and power, aiming at doing as many things as possible, rather than at the pleasure that men and women may have in doing such things. Things *are* beginning to change a little. In sociology we are beginning to see women listened to when they put forward analyses that are different from our own. When I was starting this book I noticed the great authority that Mme Simone Veil exercised in the French Government, and which she now wields in the European Parliament. And everywhere the women of the consumer associations are forces to be reckoned with.

There is fairly general agreement over the diagnosis of the ills of our society, which bears upon the obvious ascendancy of masculine values: its alienation in favour of technology, its dehumanization, and the politicization which transforms even the most generous initiatives into a vulgar struggle for power – and the excessive centralization of power which quickly corrupts those who grasp it, relegating their erstwhile virtues to the camp of the oppressed, where the vicious circle starts all over again. What, then, is the remedy? Can it be supplied by women returning to play a principal role? Sentimental effusions will not suffice.

An exchange, a dialogue, real collaboration between men and women at every level is needed to bring about fundamental change. It is much more difficult to achieve than the triumph of one sex over the other. It is clear that the question of the status of women goes far beyond the problem of equal pay. We must not confuse power with authority. Men do tend to do so, because they are always fascinated by power, and aim always at power when they alone are in authority.

57

The evidence of this is clearly seen in the evolution of our society over the last four centuries, during which men have not asked women what they think. True authority would involve rethinking the aims of civilization, of its institutions and its enterprises. The effects would be far-reaching if men and women were to set about it together. For while men are fascinated by power, women are fascinated by people and the fundamental respect their status as persons demands: respect for the weak by the powerful, for minorities by the majority, for emotional needs by those who follow abstract doctrines, and for poetry by realists.

An American woman born in Paris, Anaïs Nin, made a great impression on me in this connection. She is a poet, but lacks neither practical sense nor courage, since she herself printed her first two books in her cellar at home, because the publishers rejected them. Now they fight each other to publish her work. She asks herself 'why one writes', and answers, 'I think that one writes in order to create a world in which one can live'. And there I suddenly felt myself in accord with her. It is this transformation of our modern world through a less conventional, more intimate and personal relationship between man and woman that brings her whole book to life.

'I want this sense of the person,' she writes, 'this sense of direct contact with others, to cease being looked upon by women as a weakness. I want it to be preserved by them as a quality which could create a totally different world, in which intellect would be fused with intuition and this sense of the person.' She speaks of both a new woman and a new man, a man delivered from his fear of emotion, ready to 'recognize his sensibility', capable of 'giving way to tears', but interested as much in his home as in his business, and a woman freed from her guilt to do something other than being a good wife and looking after her children. She quotes Yoko Ono, who speaks of 'the utilization of feminine qualities as a force capable of changing the world ... of evolution rather than revolution'.

8

Hesitations

I had always thought that the emancipation of women in the West had come about progressively, the pace varying in different countries, of course, but in one continuous movement. A book by the American Betty Friedan, *The Feminine Mystique*, showed me how wrong I was. It was a book I liked because it was personal. In it she describes the evolution in the United States of ideas about the role of women, in terms of her own hesitations and changes of opinion.

She describes three periods which contrast with each other as sharply as the three bands of colour – red-white-red – on the Austrian flag! First there is the great feminist saga of the first half of this century, which as well as votes for women claimed the right to equal access with men to higher education and to any career whatsoever. It must be recognized that the reason why men in the last century refused women the opportunity of higher education was not that they judged them incapable, but deliberately to keep them under their domination and at their service: 'You ought to abhor the idea of education for girls,' wrote Balzac. 'To allow a woman to read any book she chooses, is to teach her to do without you.' (Quoted by Benoîte Groult.)

I remember seeing Ibsen's *The Doll's House* in my youth. It caused a storm of controversy. In it the claims of women were symbolized in the character of Nora, who departed, banging the door behind her, to seek freedom. Women were suddenly realizing that they had been imprisoned in the name of their duty as wives and mothers. Soon young women were invading the universities, prolonging their education, delaying marriage: they wanted to equip themselves first for a career, and then have fewer children so as to take up their career as soon as possible.

But then, quite suddenly, after 1945, with the war over, there came the second period, which Betty Friedan calls the period of the feminine mystique. (Modern feminists would prefer to speak of the feminine 'trap' – they are fond of the word.) What happened was that a veritable mystique of marriage and the home took hold of the United States. This was the counter-offensive which asserted that the feminist aim of public action to turn women away from their true destiny was an extravagant fancy. 'Modern woman's participation in politics,' it was said, 'is through her role as wife and mother.'

Betty Friedan followed the movement, gave up a bursary she had just won, married and had children. At that time, she says, the average marriage age of women in America dropped to twenty, and was still dropping... The number of American women with three or more children doubled in twenty years... The birthrate was overtaking India's... A well-known women's college adopted the defensive slogan: 'We educate women, not to turn them into scientists, but to make them wives and mothers'... The chemistry course had to be replaced by a course in advanced cooking... Two women students out of three were leaving university before the end of their courses, and in an opinion poll, 70% of them admitted that what they were looking for at university was a husband.

For those young women, says Betty Friedan, 'feminism had become ancient history'. This is confirmed by the French sociologist Evelyne Sullerot, who had two books refused by American publishers on the grounds that 'feminism is no longer in fashion'. It was indeed a matter of fashion. This was the period of sumptuous suburban villas, little palaces for the home-centred wife who had fled from the work-a-day city. They took their children by car to school in the morning, drove to fetch them back in the afternoon, in a closed circuit outside of which they hardly ever ventured. Women's magazines were filled with advice on what to do in the house, on changing the curtains and the wallpaper, recipes, child psychology, and how to please one's husband.

But then the third period arrived, and it seems probable that Betty Friedan, and the enormous success of her book, had much to do with bringing it about. In any case, for her it was like a sort of conversion: '... on an April mörning in 1959 ... the problem that had no name ...' she writes. But she soon gave a name to the unease that was attacking her – it was boredom. 'In the end it was like being in a theatre where there was nothing but intervals.' All at once she was seized by nostalgia for a more active life. Was not such an aspiration legitimate and natural? 'I no longer need to be ashamed of wanting something different', she said to herself.

Many more women were saying it too. 'We suddenly realized that all those women at home with their three and a half children were miserably unhappy!' And Margaret Mead, whose brilliant career as an ethologist dazzled them, ironically called their mode of life 'the return of the cave-woman'. So Betty Friedan went back to her studies at the university.

In reality it was not her studies that gave her a new life, but the fact that she at once became a leader, and that large numbers of enthusiastic women joined her in founding a movement, for which she found a name: she tells amusingly that in the exhaustion and excitement of the inaugural meeting she found herself spontaneously tracing the three letters NOW. Obviously that stood for a New Organization of Women, but it was also a word, and to say 'now' is to commit oneself to the future.

I could go on giving quotations which testify to the fact that a woman's dedication to her husband, her children, and her house is not enough for her fulfilment. Esther Vilar does not deal tenderly with the woman in the home: in her eyes, it is not her husband who is exploiting her, but she who is exploiting her husband. She marries only in order to ensure her keep, and still complains that 'at home she is bored'. Others go further: Léon Eisenberg quotes a trenchant remark by Jessie Bernard: 'Being housewives makes women ill.' In Claude Maillard's book, a woman declares, 'What is hard is to see the other person living'... 'Living with another person is not an end in itself. The couple is an impasse.' And another: 'What I have come to realize is that the communal mill is fed by individual mills. So long as my mill is not working, nothing will work for anyone.' So it is the very success of home life which is invoked by these women in exhorting others to break free from its too narrow limits.

I admit that Betty Friedan's description of these three successive contradictory movements impressed me. And yet I know well that we are all – men as well as women, and in Europe as much as in America – far less free in our choices than we imagine, much more conditioned by social pressure and suggestion. Such pressures are ten times stronger in the midst of such a storm of passionate and irreconcilable arguments, made all the fiercer by the power of the mass media.

It is disturbing to see women tossed about like that, so that their apparently greater liberty is in reality compromised. It is not just that influences alternate in time in the way that Betty Friedan rather simplistically describes them, drawing on her own experiences. The two views confront each other just as radically every day, to the bewilderment of women.

You will see that it is a delicate personal problem. Being a person means assuming responsibility for oneself, responding to one's inner vocation, freely choosing one's goals in life, and the routes one wishes to take to achieve them. But where is liberty? Strong personalities like Betty Friedan make their choices in accordance with their convictions, but also in accordance with their temperaments. They recount their own experiences, and whether they wish it or not, carry others with them, and start a fashion. And amid the torrent of propaganda, enthusiasm, and movements, countless women are carried along, less and less capable of making a really personal choice of their own.

Inevitably, in order to achieve liberation, they are enrolled and organized. In their organizations they experience moments of exaltation and emotional fellowship, the moving echoes of which I find in their books. But at the same time they risk losing their critical sense. They are militants – the very word involves the notion of submission to a leader. This is a problem which has always concerned me – the problem of freedom of opinion, since it is the essential attribute of the person. I have already quoted a remark made by one of my patients: 'We are always the prisoners of our liberators.'

The little village where I live was submerged for more than a century in the ebb and flow of the war between Geneva and Savoy. When the Savoyards were too threatening, Geneva called on the Bernese for help. They liberated the village, suppressed the Mass and reinstated the Lord's Supper. Then they went away and the Savoyards returned to liberate the village from the heretics and re-establish the Mass. Until the Bernese came back... The world is like that – plenty of liberations, but very little liberty.

Only once since Roman times has my little city of Geneva experienced foreign occupation. That was when the French revolutionary armies took it in the name of liberty, singing the Marseillaise! Actually men are always claiming liberty for themselves while denying it to others. Revolutionaries overthrow a tyranny, to become tyrants themselves. The aim of every political struggle, though ostensibly a campaign of liberation, is always the same – to achieve power. The first stage in the establishment of democracy is preventing a minority from oppressing the majority; but the second stage, which is more difficult to realize, is preventing the majority from oppressing minorities. Even apart from war and politics, everyone constantly tries to regulate the behaviour of others, telling them what is right, or what is good for them.

I think it even worse that people should try to impose on others a choice between two powerful and natural desires. The fact is that women want both marriage, motherhood, to love, feed, and care for their little intimate world, to have it to themselves, and at the same time to escape from its narrow limits, to open doors and windows on the world outside and share in the living community. It is scarcely ever really possible to reconcile these two desires; one or the other must be repressed. But the day comes when malaise, boredom, or, more consciously, nostalgia, manifest themselves. Such inner conflicts give rise to feelings of frustration and guilt. The woman in the home has a bad conscience about not using the talents she has been endowed with, while the working mother worries about neglecting her children. Similarly, the spinster envies the married woman's happy family life, while the latter envies the single woman's liberty. The most truly free of all is perhaps the nun, bound by her vows!

My grandmother whom I mentioned just now had no such worries. She had only one model, to which she conformed easily, and which with a clear conscience she called her duty. There were other models, such as that of the adventuress, but that did not concern her. No woman felt frustrated by not having a career, in a situation where none worked except from financial necessity. The need to participate actively in economic life was thoroughly repressed. I am glad that the modern woman has recognized that need in herself, but I see her paying dearly for her liberation.

The modern woman has plenty of models before her, and she cannot follow any one of them without the risk of hankering after the privileges attaching to another. Life is indeed full of difficult choices: to live is to choose, and to choose is always to renounce something – for a man as well as for a woman. Choosing one woman as a wife means renouncing all the others, and that is no small matter for any man. Moreover, every man lives in a state of tension between the demands of his job and those of his family. But he copes with it better – often by not even being aware of it, while his wife and children suffer for it.

It is quite a different matter for the woman! The call of the home resides tenaciously in her very flesh. The women whose books I have been reading do not like us to talk about their maternal instinct, because biology has been too often invoked to justify abuses. Nor do they talk about their hearts, but they do talk a lot about their guts. They 'feel things in their guts', they experience physical unease, they suffer all kinds of functional disturbances. These women today are freer, but they are a prey to a certain distress which doctors clearly observe, and which is very understandable. As Jean-Paul Sartre demonstrated, anxiety always results from having to face a necessary but impossible choice. That perhaps is why there are more women than men in the psychotherapist's consulting room.

They come because this endless and vehement debate is tearing them apart. The invocation of ethical principles, or even of texts from Holy Writ, as 'decisive arguments', only makes more dramatic the conflict of conscience, each side selecting what lends support to its own thesis. Personal testimony on one side or the other, however sincere, plays its part in making matters worse.

For example, alongside Betty Friedan's book which I have quoted, we may place that of another American, Marabel Morgan, entitled *The Total Woman*, which was equally successful in the United States. She recounts, not without humour, how her husband dazzled her with his talk when he was courting her, but after they had been married for a while he became completely taciturn. That happens to many couples.

One day she came to the conclusion that the reason her husband no longer talked to her was that he felt her to be tense and irritated by things in him of which she disapproved. She was not accepting him as he was. There I admire her. But she draws the following conclusion: 'A total woman' – such is the model she proposes – 'caters to her man's special quirks, whether it be in salads, sex, or sports.' And further on: 'The next time he makes a suggestion, respond if at all possible with an enthusiastic "Yes, let's!"'

If I understand properly, that means complete capitulation, the very opposite of the claims of the feminists, and in a categorical form which I do not remember having met elsewhere. She repeats several times: 'It pays.' And she shows that it works: not only did their conjugal bliss become cloudless, but their happiness was contagious. All the married couples in her husband's football club adopted her system, with the result that their team won the world championship. Jolly good for them, but for my part I should not have wanted to marry a woman who was so little of a person on her own account.

Yes, my wife accepted me, and I felt it. But when she did not agree with me she told me so clearly and sometimes explosively. This led us to take a different road to happiness, that of dialogue. The sky is not cloudless along that road, but it is a factor of growth for each of the partners. Was it not dialogue that was missing when Marabel Morgan was tense, irritated, and silent? Nevertheless, in justice it must be said that her book abounds in observations and advice full of wisdom.

It was not her husband who exacted that sort of submission from Marabel Morgan. She adopted it freely herself, as a person. There is a certain paradox here: of her own accord she chose once and for all to stifle her personal reactions.

It also has a certain grandeur. But is she accomplishing her mission, in the sense in which I use the word in this book? She lets her husband decide everything, do anything he likes. Is not this willing submission precisely the course adopted by women in past centuries? We are seeing now the result of that – a masculine world that functions like a piece of machinery, with no regard paid to emotional reactions.

Our grandmothers did not imagine it possible to adopt any other attitude, since there was no other model to follow. Whereas Marabel Morgan knows that she could act differently, and she would certainly have the courage to do so. She herself says, 'I am by nature rather dictatorial.' That is perhaps the key to the book: it is those who are naturally dictatorial who have most to gain from the experience of abdication. However that may be, my reaction to this book was to reflect that I should have been rather humiliated if my wife had adopted such a tactic, and if she alone had deserved the credit for our mutual understanding. On reflection, I am prouder than Mr Morgan.

Men are indeed very proud, and that is just what makes the problem of women more complicated. Men find being challenged hard to bear, but they find it just as hard to know that they are being handled with kid gloves. Women are well aware of this, and do not dare to say so. Perhaps it needs a man to say it. But of course I am prompted by my pride in wanting to be that man. I realized a long time ago that you cannot avoid pride. You take just as much pride in confessing it as in concealing it. And I fear that the boldest of women, those who, like Kate Millett, denounce the pride of the male, do more to exacerbate it than to exorcise it.

However, it is important to see that it was their pride in themselves that prompted men to relegate women for centuries to the corridors of history, to try to build on their own, in their own fashion, their own rational and technological civilization; and that men have been hurt by the emancipation of women, wrested from them, as it has been, by sheer force. One reaction we are seeing is their resignation as fathers from their role in the upbringing of children.

A mother was consulting me about her child; she was explaining her case most intelligently. I was able to talk about it with her as I would with a fellow doctor. She had read books, attended lectures, followed a course for parents. At the end I asked her, 'What does your husband say?' – 'Oh, he never says anything! I've tried to talk to him about it, but it's no use.' It is as if the husband had thought: Since you've made yourself such an expert, sort it out yourself, I'm having nothing more to do with it. Unconsciously, his reaction is one of resentment against his wife.

9

The Question of Value

I have referred to the wave of opinion which broke upon the United States after the Second World War. Suddenly it was being asserted that it was neither in education nor in a career that a woman's value in society lay, but rather in her irreplaceable role as wife and mother, as Betty Friedan wrote. What struck me most was her revelation of the part played by industrial strategy in this propaganda.

She does say that the loneliness of the war years had, for the girls, 'added an extra urgency to their search for love'. But she maintains that with the coming of peace, industry in the USA had to operate a difficult conversion to peace-time products, and find new outlets for them. 'In the fifties came the revolutionary discovery of the teenage market.' The housewives' market, too, of course, for the sale of all kinds of household appliances. Doubtless there was not enough there to absorb the whole output of all the industries that were casting about for markets; but it is the procedure that interests me. How did it operate?

'I learned how ...' writes Betty Friedan, 'when I went to see a man who is paid approximately a million dollars a year for his professional services in manipulating the emotions of American women to serve the needs of business.' She goes on to quote the following remark by an expert in such matters: 'We sell them what they ought to want, speed up the unconscious, move it along.' There we have a practical application of depth psychology! And this instruction to salesmen: 'The appeal should emphasise the fact that X Mix aids the woman in expressing her creativity because it takes the drudgery away ...'; that 'it permits her to use at home all the faculties that she would display in an outside career.' Our author concludes with the words of one young housewife: 'It's nice to be modern – it's like running a factory in which you have the latest machinery.'

This is all very unpleasant to learn. According to Betty Friedan the law of the world of things, the law of profit, is still pulling the strings. Behind our discussions of principle are hidden influences which are by no means disinterested. Women's freedom of choice is limited not only by a host of prejudices, but also by the deliberate intervention of businessmen. One is reminded of the case of Henry Ford, mentioned by Denis de Rougemont, who artificially created the 'need' for the motor car.

One day in an exhibition I was the target of one of these demonstrators, a virtuoso in sales talk, and I came away with a highly sophisticated mixer. I thought it would be just the gift for Nelly; but she never used it! Recently, being now on my own, I took it from the cupboard. The mechanics of it interest me: it is most ingenious – perhaps too much so. The time saved in using it is largely lost in setting up and dismantling the parts and all the accessories, cleaning them, and especially in studying the instructions, which are translated from the English into something like that word-for-word translation from German which we Swiss call 'federal French', lacking both elegance and clarity. Kate Millett writes, 'The invention of labour-saving devices has had no appreciable effect on the duration, even if it has affected the quality of their drudgery.'

As you see, all this brings us back to some very practical problems which are of great importance in the argument, in particular the boredom of household tasks. Naturally, men suggest technological solutions. But the fact that a woman works not for things but for persons, means also that she likes to work personally; that is to say, with her fingers rather than by means of a machine. That is why women persist in knitting by hand when it is much easier to go out and buy a cheap factory-made pullover. Often, when lecturing to female audiences, I tell them I don't mind if they knit while they listen to me, because I know it helps them to listen. There are always some who thereupon open their bags and take out some article to get on with. The wife of a French surgeon of my acquaintance knits throughout the conferences on the medicine of the person, and such is the atmosphere of mutual understanding there that even the men do not mind.

Note also that, working for persons rather than things, a woman spends some time thinking about the persons. One can be too scientific about the time spent on household tasks. Esther Vilar maintains that for a family of four persons it is exactly two

68

hours forty-six minutes. The time spent in thinking ought to be included.

The fact that men look upon housework as unimportant is one of the chief reasons why women find it boring and wearisome. It is important that women should feel that men appreciate what they do, and *vice versa*: each gives value to the activity of the other. I often think how unwise men are to belittle housework, and to be so frugal in their praise and so ungrateful for what the housewife does. 'You spend an hour or an hour and a half preparing a meal,' a woman says, 'and then it is all gone in a quarter of an hour, and no one says so much as thank-you for it!' No one? Sometimes the children, more spontaneous than their elders, clap their hands when Mum has prepared their favourite dish. They have not yet learned to repress their feelings.

If a man really understood, as those children do, that a woman works for people, he would also understand that it is her love for him that makes the work she does worthwhile. And if she felt she was understood and appreciated in this way, she would put all her heart and soul into her household activities. I have been told of an inter-faculty round-table conference that took place in the University of Berne on the theme of progress. It was the mathematician who had the last word: 'In the end, the only thing that matters is love!'

Jesus himself cooked a meal for his disciples while they were doing their work as fishermen (John 21.9). And that was after his resurrection, when he might well have been less concerned with earthly matters. I often think of that when I am doing my own cooking, even though I am doing it only for myself. I feel I am returning to the sources which protect me against intellectual distortion, communicating with our most distant ancestors. For after all the lesson of Prometheus is there: fire has been used for cooking as well as for forging tools – in fact the use of fire is one of the characteristics of the human species: at that point we are equal, both women and men. I find pleasure too in doing my shopping. But no doubt I am wrong to have recourse too often to the facilities of the super-market, when the real market in the street is much more personal.

In any case, things have begun to change in the matter of domestic chores. Many young couples share them equally, and find in this a quite new comradeship, which is very good for personal contact. The old prejudice is dying, that such work is demeaning to a man, as if his dignity depended on what he does rather than what he is. Such a prejudice reveals him as being both lazy and pretentious.

So what? Is there no scale of value applicable to our diverse activities? Is it a matter of indifference that we do this rather than that, that a woman stays at home or goes out to work? Is it an illusion when feminists assert that she is validated by having a job? I certainly do not think so! What really matters is that strictly subjective thing we call personal vocation, that a woman should live the life she has herself decided upon and which she is convinced is right for her. The trouble is that no one is free from the prejudices of his time, nor even, as we have seen, from hidden influences that have their own axe to grind.

The fact is that we are all constantly seeking to validate ourselves through the approval and esteem of others. When the only women to go out to work were those of modest means, the remainder sought validation in marriage. This is still to some extent true today. It is not only for love and to have a family that a woman marries. It is also because of the social status marriage confers. Parents are not oblivious of this either, even if the fiancé does not come up to what they dreamed of. Unmarried women are well aware of it, as they see married women more highly honoured merely because they are married, and not because of any real merit.

It is public opinion, too, which considers a chemist, for instance, more estimable than a cook, yet both spend their time heating, evaporating, distilling, filtering, pounding, and mixing. That is possibly the answer to the question raised by Evelyne Sullerot, as to why chemistry is the sole branch of technology which attracts women in any considerable numbers. I think that the reason for the greater prestige of chemistry is that it partakes of the prestige of science, even though cookery requires more personal skill.

Evelyne Sullerot also points out that the more women there are in an occupation, the lower the wages are. It seems then that though having an occupation validates a woman, women devalue an occupation. There is an interrelation between the two factors of function and person. Function is a masculine criterion, and the person a feminine one. Is it the function which validates the person, or the other way round? I do not know.

Everything is relative. A woman is devalued by not going on to higher education only because there are some that do. Women claimed the right to study at a time when the prestige of science was at its highest. Now it is in decline. Is that due to the atomic bomb?

Although there the scientists have been manipulated by the politicians and the military. The prestige of sociology, biology, and psychology seems to be increasing, while that of the exact sciences and the humanities is decreasing. It is the prestige of science which has always attracted more students, and it is apparently because of their numbers that it has become tarnished. In circles in which young people once thought themselves obliged to go to university, many are now declining to do so. An American doctor friend who works among students has told me that for some years now the numbers of white students at his university have been declining, while there are growing numbers of black students, who are still seeking validation in this way.

It seems to be a fact that validation for women through higher education and science seems to be in decline. They have begun to suspect this themselves. As David Riesman points out, women abandon their studies either to get married, or because they fear that too much education is a 'marriage bar'. Are they not told (Betty Friedan adds): 'If your husband is going to be an organization man, you can't be too educated'? And since more of the higher positions are reserved for men, women earn more from less learned activities.

The fact is that level of earning is taking over from level of education as a criterion of validation. It is even almost the sole factor for large numbers of unmarried women, more important than their traditional devotion to others. Is there someone sick in the family, are there children whose working mother cannot give them sufficient attention? The spinster steps into the gap, and that is looked upon as entirely normal, since she has no husband or children of her own to look after. Michèle Perrein pays them a rare tribute: it is in these 'old maids' that one finds a love that is unsurpassed in its breadth and disinterestedness, unpossessive and undemanding. All this, however, earns them very little in the way of social esteem.

On the other hand, to earn enough money to be able to instal themselves in a smart studio, artistically furnished, and boasting the latest Hi-Fi 'music centre', and to entertain lots of friends there, is a very valid compensation for their emotional deprivation. Even without a husband it is still a home, and a woman identifies with her home. This is of course why women protest so strongly against unequal pay. A woman comes off even better if she can achieve a position of independence with regard to her work. In Switzerland an

71

institution set up to this end by women's organizations has rendered great service.

But financial autonomy is also important for the married woman. All the evidence points to this. It is frequently what drives her to work despite the excessive strain imposed by her two roles, rather than the pleasure she derives from the job, which is often more tedious than her housework. 'The real curse of women,' writes Gisèle Halimi, 'is having to spend the money earned by someone else.' He who pays the piper calls the tune, even if the husband has no inkling of the power conferred upon him by his wife having to beg the smallest sum from him. A double wage means a lot more freedom in the conjugal dialogue!

But this is the moment to repeat that one is the prisoner of one's liberator. A woman's earnings procure for her a standard of life to which she becomes accustomed, and this prevents her from leaving her work if ever she decides she wants to spend more time with her children. And then, the husband's reactions have to be taken into account. Claude Maillard tells of a young woman who made it a condition of her marriage that she should have her own job. 'He agreed. But once we were married he completely changed his mind.' It happens not infrequently, I suspect, and arises from the fact that once he is married the husband comes to feel that his wife belongs to him and must devote herself entirely to him. Anaïs Nin tells of another, more liberal-minded husband, who had accepted this arrangement with his wife. This time it was she who changed her mind, because she was afraid he might think that she wanted to work because she did not love him enough.

You see how complex are all the problems raised by the emancipation of women from the home, as well as those which bind her to it! How rash it is to try to lay down the law about them. Among all the women whose books I have read on the subject, those whom I found most sympathetic were not those who were the most categorical in their views, however sincere the conviction with which those views were held, but those who admitted their own doubts. We have seen how Betty Friedan changed her mind, swinging first to one side, then to another. A writer who seemed to me to be much more perceptive, much more sensitive to her own inner conflict, was a Frenchwoman, Christiane Collange, in her book *Je veux rentrer à la maison* ('I want to go back home').

She admits right away that she wanted the best of both worlds: family and career. Even as a child she used to say, 'I want to be a journalist, and have lots of children'. And in fact she became a top-class journalist, leader-writer for a periodical of repute, and she had three sons. But she does not attempt to hide how difficult and even unsatisfying it was to play both roles at once, despite the exceptional richness of such an existence. And she points out that it would have been impossible if she had not had the privilege, so rare nowadays, of having a stable and qualified help in the home.

Even that does not solve the problem. Nor does careful organization of one's time and affairs, of which she wrote in a previous book, *Madame et le management.* For the problem is in the heart. 'The demon of the home had already been tormenting me,' she writes, 'when my last son was born... A last child is like a last love.' 'At the time,' she adds, 'my reason silenced my guts... If you stopped now, you'd rue it when you are forty... Once the children have gone, life still stretches a long way ahead.'

But the guts, as she puts it, are tenacious! She did not give in, she did not capitulate to them completely, but she came to terms. She turned down offers of jobs that were 'more prestigious, better paid', in order to get back some liberty for her home. Naturally she has incurred criticism from the feminists, as I have seen from an interview she gave. She seems to them to have betrayed the cause of women. Nevertheless she recalls how hard she fought for the married woman's right to work, the enquiries she conducted as a journalist in various countries, and points out that she still remains a supporter of the women's movement.

What I admired in this intelligent woman was her sensitivity. For example, her allusion to the drama occasioned by the slightest illness of one of her children. She does not suggest a compromise – part-time work – as an ideal solution, valid for all married women, but simply as the least bad solution in her own personal case.

You see how difficult it all is, how complex, delicate, and difficult to dogmatize about. There are women who married young, who have given up any idea of a career in order to devote themselves to their homes; and when the children are grown up, particularly when the last one marries or leaves home, they find themselves jobless and untrained. What are they do to? Mature studies? A difficult apprenticeship? Charitable work, which many people do not take seriously? Full or part time? Others at the cost of serious overwork, have taken up their career once more as soon as the youngest child reaches school age, and may later have a guilty conscience, wondering whether they have not sacrificed children and husband

73

to personal ambition.

You will realize that from the start I have declined to give advice. Recognizing a woman as a person means leaving to her the complete responsibility for her own choices; it means respecting her liberty. But what of the husband? He cannot on that account withdraw into an attitude of resignation: 'It's your business, do what you like.' We discussed this at the last conference on the medicine of the person, in Frascati. Several wives said how much they had been helped in seeking their own decisions by a conjugal dialogue which respected their consciences but which was frank and fully committed. Several said that it was their husband who had realized, before they did, that their life in the future was going to be impoverished.

This conjugal dialogue is the fundamental thing, right from the start of the marriage. It is not so much a matter of discussions about principles, as the controversialists claim, but of an honest search, step by step, for the most just line of conduct, or as I would put it, for God's will for both partners. As Christiane Collange says with great good sense about women's work, it is a matter of dosage: with one child it is still all right, with two it is not just doubly difficult, but ten times more so; with three, it is no longer possible.

This of course raises the question of family planning, which she does not discuss – and nor shall I, since it is beyond the scope of this book. The question of abortion is even further from my theme, but I ought to allude to it briefly, since the feminists make its 'decriminalization' one of their essential demands.

What is relevant to the perspectives of this book is to underline the importance of the subjective, emotional, affective factors. I believe this to be what lies behind the passion with which this claim is pressed. It is their indignation at the complete and unfair impunity of the man, who is the truly responsible party. Whether it be a youth who has seduced a girl, or a selfish husband who refuses the responsibility of one more child, it is a man who opposes any serious dialogue and who shrugs it off with 'That's your look-out!', or even without saying anything at all.

The law then seems to the woman to be like a great inexorable machine, invented by men, obeying its own logic without any care for emotional reactions. Furthermore it casts the blame on the woman, because that is easier than blaming the man, who has disappeared.

My own experience is that more often than is supposed, one can help a woman to keep her child if one talks seriously with her, even from the purely psychological point of view. No pregnant woman can fail to be sensitive to the fact that it is a life that is developing within her. Abortion always leaves a serious wound in her heart. A wound to the healing of which, moreover, I apply myself by recalling that the forgiveness of God that the Bible speaks of is unconditional; that Jesus never stopped denouncing the moralistic hypocrisy of the 'righteous', whose sin is no less serious than the one they are stigmatizing in others.

I drew down upon myself the censure of a certain personality in my church for signing a manifesto against abortion on the occasion of a Federal poll submitting to the nation a proposed compromise law which had been laboriously drawn up, but which was no solution to this insoluble problem. But I think that the feminists do not realize the sufferings which they would be imposing on women with the legalization of abortion on demand. An old friend of mine, Dr Ernst, of Ulm, has founded an international association of doctors who are against this liberalization.

10

Reflections

I have been talking about Madame Christiane Collange and her book *Je Veux rentrer à la maison*. Just when I was writing those pages, I learned from my local press that another woman, Madame Gabrielle Nanchen, a Deputy for the canton of Valais in the Federal Parliament, had decided not to be a candidate in the next elections. So she too wanted to 'go back home', to devote herself to her home, to her husband, and especially to her three children. The same sudden halt, this time to a parliamentary career.

Without any doubt she would have been re-elected, since she is held in high esteem. A 'leading spirit' in her party, as the newspaper described her, and also in the women's movement in Switzerland. The parliamentary correspondent paid her this tribute: 'Gabrielle Nanchen quickly imposed herself as one of the best deputies in the Socialist group and in the whole Parliament. She was capable of taking up any portfolio. But it is in social affairs that she will be seen to have excelled most particularly: old age and widows' pensions; maternity benefit; and so many more ...' And he went on, 'Then there was the Gabrielle Nanchen charm. The graceful figure. The exceptionally good broadcasting voice.'

There was quite a stir, of course, among the feminists. A woman journalist questions her. 'Of course,' she replies, 'there will be those who will say that my withdrawal proves that true equality is not possible. It is still true today that a man in my position would not have taken the same decision as I have. Nevertheless I think I have proved over the last eight years that a political career is compatible with family life. Don't forget that I had two very young children when I joined the Cabinet; I have been able to fulfil my two roles without letting my party down or harming my children.'

You see, she affirms both that it is possible to reconcile the two roles, and that she is no longer going to do so. It is true, you will have realized, that there is now a third child, which confirms Christiane

Collange's remark which I quoted just now. There is a misunderstanding over this word 'equality'. Equality of rights, of course.
But rights are not everything; there is the heart – or the guts, as
the feminists say. So that equality of circumstances will never be
complete.

In any case, might not the decision of this mother be considered as
a victory for feminism, just like that which she took eight years ago
to accept a parliamentary mandate? Is not a woman's right her right
to decide for herself, in spite of political pressures and all kinds of
prejudice? Is it not true emancipation to be recognized as a free and
responsible person? Basically, Gabrielle Nanchen has twice upset
people's prejudices – eight years ago it was the prejudice which says
that a mother of young children should stay at home; and now it is
the prejudice of the feminists who regard the abandonment of her
political mandate as a betrayal.

You will understand that I am seeking here to transfer the
argument to a more essential level. The important thing is not
to dictate to women what they ought to do, but to respect their
freedom; to trust them, to invite them to reflect upon their mission,
upon the contribution they feel called to make to our civilization at
this time of crisis, wherever they are, in Parliament or in their
families. It is somewhat ridiculous to count the number of women
who enter Parliament, take part in government or some other
official activity, as if one were keeping the score at a match, and to
use that as a measure of the emancipation of women. Of course, at
the start, their entry into professional or political life marked a
notable breakthrough. But now it is no longer necessary for them to
prove their capabilities.

The fact that there are still very few women in parliaments and in
governments is in my view not so much due to old prejudices. It is
rather because of the manifest difficulty of reconciling a political
career with their maternal task and their own feelings. Single
women would be more available, but I am very much afraid that in a
mixed assembly such as a parliament they would not carry as much
weight as their married sisters. Men do not take them as seriously as
they do married women. The political parties are obviously aware of
this, since they always state in their election addresses the number
of children that each woman candidate has.

However that may be, I hope that women will exercise an increasingly beneficial influence on the development of our civilization,
but I doubt whether it is going to be to any large extent through their

participation in politics, where what counts is the weight of each group. If you have ten kilograms on one side of the balance and a few grams on the other, adding a few more grams, or even a kilogram or two, will make no difference. You have got to go up to ten kilograms to make the balance swing.

This, I think, is the explanation of why the giving of the vote to women and allowing them to stand for election has had so little effect on politics. Women have had to fit themselves into the typically masculine mould of the parliamentary system, with its interminable arguments about principles and its set-piece debates between the parties. In real life, on the other hand, a woman can carry her full weight, because it does not depend so much on her function as on her person. It is men who pay more attention to the function than to the person.

I could give many examples. At this very moment local elections are being held in my town. Madame Lise Girardin has also decided not to stand again. She was the first woman Mayor of Geneva; her election was hailed as a first decisive step in the political emancipation of women here, and her work was greatly appreciated. But she was the only woman, and she has now been replaced by a man.

Are we to see in her case, in those of Christiane Collange and Gabrielle Nanchen, in the success of Marabel Morgan in the USA, and in a number of other obvious signs, evidence of a certain ebbing of the tide of feminism, or at least of a change of course, another climatic change rather like the one Betty Friedan described in the fifties?

Are there signs of disappointment in the feminist movement at the fact that the political and professional emancipation of women has brought so little change to the progress of our ever more technological and increasingly less humane civilization? It would be a disappointment analogous to that of the ex-colonial nations who have also gone along with this Western civilization, at the risk of the loss of some of their own genius.

I was struck by a remark made by Evelyne Sullerot. In her introduction to the remarkable book which she edited along with Jacques Monod, entitled 'The Feminine Fact', she notes an ambiguity which weighs upon the feminist movement. On the one hand, claiming for women the same rights as for men, it tends to deny the biological and psychological differences that distinguish them from men; and on the other, it sets out to stress their personal originality: 'What do we want,' she wonders, ' – to make ourselves more like men, or to express our own specific character as women?'

It seems to me that this contradiction can be resolved if we distinguish two successive phases. At the start of the movement for women's emancipation it was necessary for women to show that they were as capable as men of taking on the tasks which had been denied them. It was necessary therefore to insist on the first term of the dilemma – the similarity of men and women. Now, however, the capability of women has been proved, even though they are still a long way from achieving complete emancipation. It is time, therefore, to stress the second term of the dilemma, and to ask if there is something that we can expect of women which men are less capable of providing. To see victory for feminism only in terms of a woman assuming a function like a man, will do no more than confirm the prejudice of masculine superiority, since it is to take man as the model. As France Quéré puts it, 'We want a woman to be a person, but we ask her to act like an ape – aping men, to whose superiority we thus pay homage.'

Similarly, Régine Pernoud, the historian whom I quoted in connection with the Middle Ages, writes: 'It is as if women, delighted with the idea of having penetrated the masculine world, remained incapable of the extra effort of imagination they need to make in order to endow that world with their own particular character, which is the very quality that our society lacks. They are content to imitate men, to be judged capable of doing the same jobs, to adopt the manners and even the sartorial habits of their partners... One begins to wonder if they are not moved by unconscious admiration ... of a masculine world which they think it necessary and sufficient to copy as exactly as possible, even at the cost of losing their own identity and denying in advance their own originality.'

If there is indeed some disappointment perceptible in feminist books, it may derive from other factors. No adventure lasts unless it is given a new start and a fresh impetus to aim at different goals from those it began with. Every adventure gradually fades and comes to a stop, sometimes, it is true, because it has failed, but more often because of its very success. It was exciting to be the first woman doctor, the first woman barrister, the first woman army officer or head of government. But the more there are, the more ordinary it becomes. Every success, even the passing of the smallest examination, seems great in prospect and trivial in retrospect. It is like a new dress, which seems fantastic to a woman when she is dreaming of buying it, but disappointing as soon as she possesses it.

New ideas, even the most revolutionary, remind me of the bob-sleigh races which I like watching on TV. You see a competitor making an enormous effort to push off his sleigh as quickly as possible, jumping into it at the last moment; from then on he is no longer pushing, but being carried. So in every new idea there is a first very short heroic phase, demanding unremitting effort from the pioneers. But once it has begun to catch on, it carries its partisans along with it instead of being pushed by them. It becomes a recognized institution, a savourless routine. Just as it arouses great passion while it is meeting opposition, so it is emptied of passion as soon as it becomes accepted.

I believe that in every human heart there is an instinct of con-tention; so that every contestant finds pleasure, enthusiasm, and fulfilment in taking upon himself a contentious issue. You will tell me that there are conservative spirits as well – true, but they derive their pleasure from contesting the contestants: it is still a combat. Passions are more easily mobilized for war than for peace. Who can deny that the seductive attraction of contention has played an important part in the feminist movement?

Once Nelly and I were in conversation with a quite young doctor and his wife. It was a good number of years ago, at the time when young men were beginning to let their hair grow longer and when it was still looked upon as a challenge. I felt that my colleague was a little put out, as if he were surprised at the pleasure we were taking in the conversation. At last he asked us, 'Are you not shocked that I wear my hair so long?' Nelly burst out laughing, and answered, 'You are talking to one of the first women to cut their hair short in Geneva!'

It was a much more serious matter in those days! There is even a text in the Bible which praises a woman's long hair as her glory (I Cor. 11.15). Nevertheless I do not remember that we had a serious disagreement about it. Nelly saw it mainly as a practical convenience, and that pleased me. I could guess at the significance of it from the look in my father-in-law's face when he saw his daughter with an 'Eton crop'. It was obvious that she would not have dared to do it before she married me!

So it was a little feminist manifesto. No doubt it was quite un-conscious on her part, but Nelly was showing her joy at being liberated by marriage from the family tutelage. But my father-in-law did not say anything, any more than he had at the sight of the gaudy wallpapers we had chosen for our flat under the influence of the famous Paris exhibition of decorative arts that took place at that time.

More even than as feminists, we were taking up a position as critics of the bourgeois world to which we both belonged. Perhaps there was something in it of opposition to my father-in-law, for want of having been able to oppose my father, who had died. As it turned out, my father-in-law took it in good part. He trusted me wonderfully, and we remained on the most affectionate terms, enjoying a friendship which was deepened still further during his last illness. But I have always remained a rebel. I applauded the revolt of the Paris students in May 1968. And I remain so today with my criticism of our civilization.

There exists, then, a certain connivance among the various movements which challenge the *status quo*. But there is also a certain ambiguity, which comes from the fact that they tend to exploit each other. At the time of the French Revolution, women threw themselves passionately into the fray, in the hope that the liberty being proclaimed would bring with it liberation for them as well. They harangued the crowds, demanding liberty for themselves, and saying that 'the right to the guillotine meant also the right to speak'. To begin with, men took advantage of this feminine dynamism; but as soon as the Revolution had triumphed, they shut the mouths of the women. We find the same thing again today in the movement for working women's rights. In a book by Evelyne Le Garrec published in France women complain bitterly of the way in which the trade unions, after benefiting from the support of the feminists, back out when it comes to reciprocating that support.

There is, then, a certain pleasure in being 'anti' which sustains the ardour of all militants, but which is certainly insufficient to bring about a real change in public opinion. In order to rally large numbers of people to one's cause, one has to present them with a goal, a valid ideal. Scientific psychology cannot go further than that, for science ignores values. Psychology can study the dynamics of behaviour, unmask our unconscious motivations, but our authentic motives, our convictions, our scales of values, are by definition outside its scope.

It is incontestably an authentic value which has ensured the success of the feminist movement, namely justice – a value that is universally recognized, even by those who flout it, as they show by the efforts they always make to justify their injustice in the name of what they claim is a higher justice. The feminists were also able to invoke the dignity of the human person, which forbids any discrimination between the rights of men and of women. This equality is, indeed, still incomplete, both in law and in fact, though recognized at least in principle. A woman may do as she wishes – she exposes herself only to criticism.

And of course critics are never wanting, whatever she does, precisely because with her liberty she is constrained to certain choices. One of the most unfair criticisms made, in my view, is that she is perverting her nature, denying her maternal instinct. Instincts are immutable. Are we expected to believe that it was only a woman's maternal instinct that kept her tied to the hearth, and not the dictates of men? In any case the middle-class woman in the past had less to do with her children then modern mothers do. They handed them over to the care of servants. There is a lot of hypocrisy in all these arguments.

All psychologists know, moreover, that the maternal instinct can become the source of a possessiveness that is harmful to the child's development when he grows up and must break away from his mother. This break is all the harder to accept if the mother has intensely enjoyed being all in all to and for her child. She goes on treating him like a baby, jealous of any other influence, and denying him everything that contains some element of risk. Once past the first few years, during which the mother's solicitude is indispensable, it is not at all proved that children suffer from the activities of the mother outside the family. Betty Friedan remarks that Russian children whose mothers go out to work are more stable than American children.

What a child needs is love, a superior quality of love, disinterested love. It can happen that a mother who has little time to spare for her child has a much more fruitful relationship with him because she is herself more of a whole person, more ready to give of herself, more generous. That is the basic problem, and it has less to do with the life the mother leads than with her inner state, less to do with doing than with being. It has to do with the theme of this book, with a sense of the person and with personal contact, to which women are predisposed by their nature, but which they need to cultivate.

Other critics say mockingly that a woman is never satisfied; she is bored at home, and when she is at work she misses her home! As if men did not get just as bored as women, or were better able to put up with boredom, when it seems to me that the contrary is the case. In the country a man misses the town and its bustling distractions, and in the town he longs for the country and its blissful peace. One always longs for what one has not got, and since all liberty involves making choices, there are always lots of things that one has not got.

The problem of boredom, however, goes deeper. I am not thinking of the nostalgia for the things one misses, but of boredom itself, the feeling of boredom. It is bound up with the problem of the meaning of life, and it arises as soon as what one is doing seems devoid of meaning. When women claimed the right to education and to work, it was not only on account of the work, but for the interest it gave them and the meaning it imparted to their lives. And they are often disappointed in this respect.

But here we are, with men and women equal, or nearly so, save for the fact that the highest and most interesting posts are reserved on the whole for men. But the whole of our over-systematized, over-organized society provokes boredom. The artisan used to see a meaning in his life because he could see the fruit of his work. I do not need to labour the point. But there, the second wind which I hope for for the feminist movement now that its first contentious phase is almost over, could be the ambition to cure our society of its anaemic deficiency of personal contact.

Nothing contributes more to giving a meaning to our lives than to realize that we have a mission. And the realization of our mission is closely bound up with awareness of our personal talents. I invite women to question themselves, to ask themselves if it is true that they are, as I believe, better endowed than we are for personal contact, for the emotional life, for concrete attention to the personal needs of each individual. Then, that would mean that after having dared to do a course of studies despite the attitude of men, after having dared to penetrate the men's world of work, of things, that they should also dare to become more personal, no longer to be ashamed of their sensibility, of their emotions, of their feelings, of all that is irrational in themselves and which men repress because they are afraid of it.

11

Women Speak

So feminism could enter a second phase. In the first it claimed for women the right to share in life outside the home, in society, in political, professional, and cultural life, and in part obtained it. In the second phase women would recognize their peculiar talents and consequently what it is their vocation to bring to the world, which men are less capable of providing. As we have seen, a man is at ease in the manipulation of things, in objective study and functional organization aimed at technological progress and production. He is much less at ease in the domain of affectivity, which is so essential to life, in the expression of his personal feelings, and even in the awareness of his own emotions.

The result is this cold, impersonal, machine-like world in which we live. How can women bring back some warmth into it? Surely by being more themselves, by exploring the world in their way, by feeling it in their way, by understanding life in their way – not biologically but personally – by thinking and speaking in their way. It is not an easy way to follow! For so many centuries women have taken men as their model, and have striven to be what men wanted them to be.

I think I can see the first signs of this venture. For example, in a book entitled 'In other words', in which Marie Cardinal and Annie Leclerc hold a discussion together. It does still contain bitter complaints against men and their stupidity, but that is not the main accent of the book. These two women are in search of themselves, of their specific quality as women. They ask what it is to write in a feminine manner. Marie Cardinal gives a reply whose importance I feel she does not appreciate: 'I do not know any more,' she says, 'I only want to write in the first person.' What does that mean? – That a woman has a sense of the person, of course! A man writes in the third person in order to express abstractions, theories, ideas, things. A woman witnesses to her personal experience. To write in the first person is to put oneself in the reader's hands, to address him personally and to establish a personal relationship with him, or at least to attempt to do so.

I was of course amused at this, because of course for a very long time I too have written in the first person, because to do so is to treat the reader not as a reading and studying machine, but as a person to talk with. That is also the reason why I write my manuscripts so carefully that I do not have to type them out for the printer. To write legibly is a sign of respect for other people as persons. This all confirms that my *anima* (in C. G. Jung's sense) is less repressed than is the case with most men. It is true, too, that in my career my sensitivity has played a bigger part than my scientific knowledge. And I am in good company. Other men have written in this way, and I like to take as an example Jean-Jacques Rousseau who touches me as a person even though I am not in agreement with his ideas. The same is true of all these books written by women which I have been reading in preparation for my own. They write in the first person, and they say what they feel – and that is what I am looking for, much more than what they think.

You will ask me what Marie Cardinal and Annie Leclerc talk about in their book. They take pleasure, for instance, in talking about the blood of their periods, and the blood of childbirth and abortion. I understand them: they are getting their own back handsomely for the centuries during which these things had to be hidden as if they were shameful. Blood is a symbol of glory – witness the blood of heroes shed for their country, the blood of the martyrs, and the blood of Jesus Christ shed for the salvation of the world, which we drink with the greatest veneration in the Communion. What about the blood of women? – It is forbidden to speak of it! – Why? I believe it is the sign of men's unconscious contempt for women. I shall be returning to this point.

Blood plays a considerable part in a woman's life, one that is magnified by the heavy silence surrounding it. The present 'pill' does not deprive a woman of her periods, though it would be perfectly possible, apparently without difficulty, to prescribe one which would suppress them. I confess that I was unaware of this. But it appears that gynaecologists will not have anything to do with it for fear of psychological reactions on the part of their patients. They know them too well! Women complain of the trouble and inconvenience of their periods, but they cling to them! It is irrational; it is a matter of sentiment.

For them their periods are an indispensable sign of their femininity; the sign, too, of their youth! That is why the menopause in women is so frequently accompanied by organic and psychological disturbances. It gives them the feeling that they are growing prematurely old, at an age when men are still in full vigour. But up to that time menstruation is a factor profoundly affecting their whole existence. It may be new for them to write about it in a book, but there can be few women who do not talk about it among themselves. They are constantly thinking about it in order to work out the date of some engagement or other. For many it is an obsessive handicap to their social life. In a previous book entitled *Parole de femme* ('A Woman's Word'), Annie Leclerc warned the reader at the outset, 'What I have to say comes from my guts'.

The ambivalent psychological attitude of women towards menstruation is general; it is the cause of all kinds of affections, not solely gynaecological. But it also means that a woman experiences her body in a different way from a man; she identifies with it more closely; she experiences her sex in the whole of her body, depending entirely on the menstrual cycle. And what are we to say about the single woman who longs to marry and have children, and yet who has to put up with all these pointless periods? Consider, however, how the lot of the married woman has changed in this respect. In the past, with eight or ten children, whom she carried for nine months and nursed for three years, she had very few useless periods, and she managed very well without them.

Blood, however, also means haemorrhage, the often alarming haemorrhage of childbirth. Birth bleeds! Caesarian births bleed even more. We are all born in a bloodbath. That is perhaps the explanation of our revulsion from blood. But the most sensational haemorrhage is that of abortion, lacking as it does the joy of bringing a child into the world. These are a woman's intensest emotions, experiences that are not only psychological, but physical as well.

Marie Cardinal relates this experience with a realism well calculated to affect a doctor: 'They thought that I was done for,' she writes, 'and they sent for Jean-Pierre to come to the operating theatre. My mind was quite clear the whole time, and from a certain moment on I was extremely happy. I could not feel my body any more, but my brain was extraordinarily active. I was paying close attention to all the people around me. It was in Canada. I could see them working with admirable professionalism. They did everything they could to save the life of this complete stranger, as I was to them. I felt love for them, because they were acting with great love, great strength, and great competence. I wanted to help them in order to show my gratitude. The next day the doctor said to me, "It is thanks to you that you pulled through; you collaborated very well." In fact I had been incapable of doing anything physical at all, I was so weak from loss of blood that I remember not being able even to raise my head. The little I did, I know very well that I did not do it in order to pull through, because I felt fine. I did it in return for what they were doing for me.'

There could be no better expression of what we doctors also feel, in psychotherapy as well as in surgery or any other specialism, the vital pact between patient and doctor, in which love is truly reciprocal and disinterested. Marie Cardinal continues: 'I was attached to a sort of high tube full of mercury which gave a constant indication of my blood-pressure. I could see the column remaining between zero and two, despite the blood transfusions – I had been given a transfusion of five litres, which is a lot. I was embarrassed for them that I wasn't doing any better than that. It is still one of the most beautiful memories of my life. I could no longer feel anything; it was as if my body was completely weightless. I had an impression of total freedom.' Annie Leclerc asks her, 'Didn't you even think "I am going to die"?' – And Marie Cardinal replies, 'Oh, yes! But I didn't mind a bit!'

What took place there was a sort of exorcism of death, of victory over death. And when we realize that human beings – because they are the only creatures who know they are going to die – live in a perpetual state of unconscious anxiety about death, we understand that what was happening was a supreme liberation. That, I think, explains the feeling she had of supreme happiness. You read what she said: 'It is still one of the most beautiful memories of my life.'

All this reminds us of the accounts collected by Dr Raymond Moody from the lips of men and women whom modern techniques of resuscitation have made it possible to bring back to life after several minutes – as many as fourteen? – of 'clinical death'. What does this expression 'clinical death' mean? They were not dead, since they were resuscitated! I did not see in Dr Moody's book any accounts of the Beyond, but rather of the feelings they experienced in the last moments as death approached, at the moment of the first steps towards the Beyond. They show us that death, so terrifying from a distance, appears beneficent from close to, when its final process begins. This is confirmed by the researches of Mme Kübler-Ross, who actually points to a misunderstanding at the last moment between the living and the dying, because the dying have already entered into a reality that is inconceivable to the living.

This means, then, that the frontier between life and death is not as precise and clear-cut as we thought. It suggests that there is a kind of no-man's-land between them. Very awkward for doctors, whose efforts to find a definition of death are brought to naught! It is curious that doctors, who are devoted to the defence of life against death, cannot achieve a definition of death.

For after all, in all the cases dealt with by Moody, without the techniques of resuscitation the moment of death would have been given as that at which recourse was had to those techniques. This must be even more awkward for the philosophers with their age-old rationalism, since it involves the negation of the principle of contradiction, which has been its basis since Aristotle: if one is alive, one is not dead, and if one is dead, one is no longer alive. It seems that what we are seeing here is a breach being made in the system of thought of the whole of the West, not dissimilar from that made in classical physics – up to that point just as hermetic – by Einstein and Heisenberg with the theory of relativity and the uncertainty principle. We all know how productive the breach in that particular logical system has been. Erich Fromm demonstrates clearly that all our Western culture rests on the three logical principles of Aristotle, that of identity (A is A), that of contradiction (A is not non-A), and that of the excluded middle (A cannot be both A and non-A). Erich Fromm refers to this in connection with love, for love is not logical. Aristotle's principles are those of correct thought, he says, not those of correct action. Now, love is action, not thought. As you see, we are getting back to the theme of this book! Our Western civilization illustrates in striking fashion the contradiction between thought and conduct: its thought – objective, scientific, logical – is perfection itself. But its conduct is inhuman. It is masculine, because it gives preference to thought over conduct. Women, for their part, do not care so much about logic as about conduct, not so much about thought as about experience.

It is true that this Western dualism does not go back only to Descartes, but right back to Aristotle, who separated physics from metaphysics – what can be proved logically, from what can be felt and lived intuitively. Man incarnates logical intelligence, woman the heart's intuition. What we need to discover is that they are complementary, and that this complementarity can be incarnated in a much more profound collaboration between man and woman. For the function of intelligence, as Descartes taught, is to divide, separate, and oppose. Only intuition leads to synthesis. Thus we men can perceive the fundamental unity of the person only by sticking the pieces together again, if I may put it so, which we have first dissected. Women, on the other hand, have a direct intuition of it.

Erich Fromm also compares Western culture with those of the East, which do give priority to intuition over thought. In the West even religion has become intellectual and dogmatic, shot through with academic controversy, intolerance, and war; whereas in the East tolerance, respect, and acceptance of others are the order of the day. This fact struck Karl Jaspers. In Japan one can choose a Shintoist celebration for one's marriage, and a Buddhist ceremony for a funeral. I talked about this with one of my interpreters, the Rev. Joseph Yamaguchi, who did his thesis for a doctorate in Catholic theology in intuition in Zen and in Bergson.

Bergson was rare among Western thinkers in attempting to re-habilitate intuition, repressed since the Renaissance in favour of reason. He wrote, 'The intellect is characterized by a natural inability to comprehend life.' Indeed, what the intellect comprehends of life is its biology, its physiological, psychological, and sociological phenomena, but not life itself. Objective study throws light on mechanisms and their interaction, but not on their cause – the 'how', not the 'why'. To explain how the genetic code works is not to discover why there is one. It is intuition which grasps mysteries. Bergson also warned of the danger of the predominance of techno-logical development, a danger which has worsened since his time. In compensation he called for a 'soul supplement', which has not come. Might it not come from women, with their greater intuition – animated by the *anima*?

We have just seen, from the dialogue between two women – very intelligent women, too – that what fascinates them is not so much the logical construction of an image of the world as what they experience and perceive personally, sensations rather than concepts. So there are two forms of comprehension, one logical and intellectual, and the other intuitive, affective, corporeal rather than cerebral. The cerebral predominates in men, and explores the 'how'; and the corporeal in women, asking 'why?'. Women have less need of intellectual formulation, simply because they are better at grasping the mysteries which no words can define.

The logical intellect gives the impression that it comprehends. Because we men understand the 'how' of mechanisms, we think we are understanding everything, and we do not think to ask women to help us to understand what we do not understand. Nevertheless that would be a real advance for women, if men realized what they lacked and looked to women to supply it. I remember one day in my prayers asking God to give me more intuition. Immediately afterwards during my meditation I realized that God had set at my side a source of intuition in the person of my wife, and that I did not listen to her enough. And not only my wife, but all the women with whom I entered into dialogue every day in my consulting room.

We find the same thing on the religious level, as Bergson also demonstrated. Of course faith presents to our minds important intellectual questions which we must study objectively; but everybody feels – and the theologians themselves constantly assert – that the logical intellect is equally powerless to comprehend the mysteries of faith as it is to understand the mysteries of life. Then the whole of theology can seem to be a gigantic effort to comprehend intellectually what cannot be so comprehended. Perhaps the same can be said of philosophy. Did not Socrates tirelessly pursue his attempt to know himself, while at the same time asserting with equal constancy that it was impossible?

One cannot read the gospels without being struck by the fact that Jesus was in general better understood by women than by men. Look, for example, at the conversations Jesus had with Nicodemus and with the Samaritan woman, which John reports in the third and fourth chapters. Nicodemus is the man, the scholar, the important personage, who pushes intellectual honesty to the point of recognizing the spiritual authority of the poor vagabond whom he comes clandestinely, but respectfully, to see: 'Rabbi,' he says to him, 'we know that you are a teacher who comes from God.' Notice in passing that he uses the 'we' of academic discourse, rather than 'I'. But he understands nothing of what Jesus says to him. When Jesus speaks of new birth, Nicodemus puts to him the scientific question 'How?': 'How can that be possible?' Jesus replies, 'You, a teacher in Israel, and you do not know these things!'

The Samaritan woman is the foreigner to whom a Jew ought not to speak, and in doing so Jesus opposes racism. She is also a woman, and when his disciples return they are 'surprised to find him speaking to a woman'. To her Jesus says things that are as difficult to understand as the things he was saying to Nicodemus: about living water which he gives, and that anyone who drinks that water 'will never be thirsty again'. She too puts the objective question 'How?' – 'How could you get this living water?' On the other hand, she understands at once when he talks to her about her personal life: 'I see you are a prophet, sir.' And she raises at once the spiritual question, about the Messiah. Jesus answers, 'I who speak to you am he.'

Jesus never declared his identity so clearly to any man. Even with his disciples he employed the method used by psychotherapists, of asking questions which awaken their intuition. 'But you, who do you say I am?' (Matt. 16.15). The apostle Peter replies, 'You are the Christ, the Son of the living God.' And yet how many misunderstandings there are between Jesus and his disciples right to the end! The last conversation he has with them, reported by John (13.31–17.26), is tragic. All their questions show that they have failed to grasp the essential meaning of his words, and in each reply that Jesus makes we feel how much this hurts him. They have misunderstood in a masculine, objective manner. They are looking for events – that he should show them the Father, that he should drive out the Romans, that he should institute his kingdom.

The same misunderstanding occurs with Pilate. 'It is you who say it. Yes, I am a king,' he answers, but not without having first asserted, 'Mine is not a kingdom of this world' (John 18.36-37). But do not forget Pilate's wife! She has assumed her mission, in the sense in which I use the word here: she has paid attention to a dream, that source of the deepest intuitions; she has understood that her husband is in danger of committing an injustice, and she does not fail to tell him so (Matt. 27.19).

Again, it was to a woman, Mary Magdalene, that Jesus first revealed his resurrection. Nothing shows more clearly the esteem and confidence he had towards women. She too understood. One eloquent detail – she understood the moment he called her by her name! Personal contact again! (John 20.16). And it is she whom he charges with the task of announcing the news to the apostles, though he must have known that those men would not be disposed to believe women: 'this story of theirs seemed pure nonsense' (Luke 24.11). That is frequently what a man says to his wife when she tells him of something about which she has an intuition: 'You are not being objective, you are imagining things!'

I could quote other examples of how Jesus took women seriously.

He treated them as persons, as people worth conversing with, worthy of his most intimate confidences. Cast your eye over the whole of history, from the earliest to the most recent times: Jesus' attitude is seen to be absolutely unique. It seems to me that not enough has been made of this obvious fact. He shows himself to be free of all prejudice: he talks to women as he does to men, with the same respect and confidence, the same demands, and the same promises. You will point out that he chose only men as his disciples. But that is because he was entrusting them with a missionary task to the multitudes which a woman would not have been able to take on in the society of his time.

It is manifest, however, that he felt the injustice of men towards women in that society. The point is made by the historian Jean Delumeau: 'Jesus willingly surrounds himself with women, talks with them, looks upon them as persons in the full sense of the word, particularly when they are despised.' Thus, he takes up the defence of a prostitute in the house of Simon the Pharisee, even holding her up to him as an example (Luke 7.36-50); he defends the adulterous woman when she is dragged before him by a mob of threatening men, sure of their right to stone her in accordance with the law of Moses (John 8.3-11); and he defends Mary, when her jealous sister Martha complains that she is spending too much time with him. The sin which Jesus denounces is the besetting sin of the 'righteous' – contempt!

The liberating influence of Jesus was enormous. In the primitive church women played a much larger part than in the society of their day. St Paul, of course, was not exempt from a certain complex about women. Nevertheless there are some biblical scholars who question the authenticity of the passage in which he lays down that they are to remain silent at meetings (I Cor. 14.34). It was, after all, St Paul who wrote that in Christ 'there are no more distinctions between ... male and female' (Gal. 3.28). There could hardly be a plainer declaration of the equality of men and women as persons. Note also how in his greetings he mentions his women friends. One last detail: the first baptism he performed in Europe was that of Lydia, a humble market-woman who sold purple dye, and he lodged at her house.

Furthermore, the Bible as a whole is more liberal in its attitude to women than other writings of the period. Deborah was a judge in Israel (Judg. 4.4), and she put herself at the head of the army alongside Barak, and defeated Sisera. There were prophetesses:

the coming of Christ was celebrated by Anna, as it was by Simeon (Luke 2.36). At Pentecost the apostle Peter quoted the words of Joel: 'Their sons and daughters shall prophesy' (Acts 2.17), acknowledging that women had a public religious role. As for the well-known misogyny of the early Fathers of the church, Eric Fuchs shows that it was due to the influence of the Stoicism of the period, and Dr Nodet attributes it to the neurosis of St Jerome. The church has paid dearly for these deviations.

Woman, writes Abbé Oraison, 'is significative of openness to transcendence'. She comprehends mysteries. It was literally through her body – her guts, as the feminists of whom I was talking earlier might say – that Elisabeth understood the mystery of the incarnation, since it was the child she was bearing in her womb, the future John the Baptist, who made her understand it by leaping within her! (Luke 1.39-45). And when she revealed the full significance of it to the Virgin Mary, her cousin, the latter uttered the Magnificat! A supreme instance of a woman speaking – the Magnificat (Luke 1.46-55).

12

Do Men Listen?

There is another book that will take us deeper into our study of Jesus' conversations with women: *L'évangile au risque de la psychanalyse*, by Françoise Dolto, in conversation with Gérard Séverin. The book is in the form of an interview, a dialogue between a man and a woman, both of them psychoanalysts practising in Paris. It was especially Françoise Dolto's truly feminine sensitivity running through the book that touched me, because she looks at certain well-known biblical scenes with a new eye, more penetrating than my masculine vision. It occurred to me that it is a pity that theology has been almost entirely the preserve of men. There are, of course, a few striking exceptions, such as St Teresa of Avila and St Teresa of Lisieux.

One of the most remarkable chapters in the book alludes to the dialogue between Jesus and his mother at the wedding in Cana (John 2.1-11), including the saying of Jesus which has always left me a little perplexed: 'Woman, why turn to me? My hour has not come yet.' It is true that there is an 'objective' argument about the hour, the hour for Jesus to 'leave a life of silence, a hidden life for a public life'. And he says that this hour has not yet arrived.

What Françoise Dolto restores to this account is the emotional dialogue which underlies the objective dialogue. The true argument is not between Jesus and his mother, but in the very heart of Jesus, which is wrung with anguish as the decisive hour approaches, and his mother, with her feminine intuition, senses it. Jesus' reply is an admission of his perturbation, and means, 'Woman, what is this sudden extraordinary reverberation within me at your words?' It takes a woman, even more than a psychoanalyst, to understand that. Jesus' remark struck me as mysterious because it is not logical. Men always try to understand by means of logic. This remark is an emotional communication.

94

But Mary is less anxious than he is, and that is why she foresees correctly that the hour has come 'in the way a mother feels that she is going to give birth'. You see, we come back to childbirth, woman's supreme emotional experience, like the feminists whom I was quoting just now! To childbirth and to blood – from the beginning of the scene Françoise Dolto sees in the wine at Cana a symbol of the blood which Jesus will shed, to be symbolized again in the wine of the Last Supper, which he will give his disciples to drink as a sign of 'the new covenant between men and God'. And straight away, in reply to Gérard Séverin's question, 'What is happening? Françoise Dolto exclaims, 'What is happening is a birth!'

So blood and childbirth are in some way for a woman the cipher stencil through which she can read the meaning of events. The event here is the birth of Jesus to his public ministry, and it is Mary who gives birth, becoming for the second time 'the mother of God'. She feels, rather than reasons, that the hour has come, and that is why she communicates her conviction to her son without words. He is about to put into practice her intuition in the miracle at Cana, in an action which arises out of the unique bond existing between mother and son, sealed indissolubly in the act of giving birth. In his mother's simple words, 'They have no wine', he has 'heard and recognized the signal from the Holy Spirit for which he was waiting'. Mary is fulfilling her woman's mission, in the meaning which I give to the word in this book. She is the initiator, discerning the will of God thanks to her woman's intuition, and she communicates her certainty to her son.

At the end of the ministry inaugurated at Cana, three days before the Passion, the anointing at Bethany (John 12.1-8) matches the scene which we have just been studying. This time it is a wordless dialogue, between Jesus and another Mary, the sister of Lazarus whom he had brought back to life. While they were having a meal together, with the disciples and possibly other guests, 'Mary brought in a pound of very costly ointment, pure nard, and with it anointed the feet of Jesus, wiping them with her hair; the house was full of the scent of the ointment'. A scene of love and of wild extravagance which attracted severe criticism, notably from Judas Iscariot.

As Françoise Dolto remarks, Mary is no longer the passive young girl sitting at Jesus' feet to listen to his words. She has become a different woman, active now, and acting without any fear of the censure of men. I add that what we see here is the emancipation

95

of a woman – she enters History, History with a capital H. She is the bearer, through intuition, of an essential message at the most decisive moment in all History. And Jesus understands her message, that the hour of his sacrifice has come. 'Perhaps without realizing it herself,' writes Françoise Dolton, 'Mary reveals to him his imminent death.' Jesus says it aloud: she poured out the perfume 'for the day of my burial'.

There is another story about the pouring out of perfume, to which I have already alluded (Luke 7.36-50). Françoise Dolto brings them together: 'These two women are expressing their love. Jesus accepts the homage of their feminine sensitivity, as they lovingly give, risking the criticism of others.' She also puts this account alongside the story of Cana: 'Just as Mary, his mother, had revealed at Cana his public hour, it is possible that Mary of Bethany with her perfume revealed, through her love and her intuition, the arrival of the hour of his death.'

You see that our idea that women have a mission in the world is taking on a new and deeper dimension. It is not just a case of women listening to Jesus – and understanding him better than many men – it is a case of women to whom Jesus listens, to whom he listens truly and intensely, hearing their message as a revelation of the will of his Father. At certain decisive moments Jesus allows himself to be led along the path that they reveal in front of him.

It is not often, I think, that men listen to women like that, with such serious expectation. What men expect mostly from women is service – sexual service, household service, teaching service in the upbringing of their children, or aesthetic services for their social life, and the services of a conscientious secretary. What they hardly look for at all is initiative, ideas, much less advice. They are usually irritated when women try to give them these things, and are not very inclined to follow them. 'My husband,' a woman says to me, 'has just made a wise decision at the suggestion of one of his friends. I gave him the same advice a long time ago, but he never listened. But as soon as his friend said it to him, he agreed.'

It seems to me that generally speaking men do not listen to women as seriously as women listen to men. We all know the positive tone in which a little girl will exclaim, 'My daddy said so'; or a wife: 'My husband said so'; a mother: 'My son said so'; and a secretary: 'My boss said so'. For these women it is an unanswerable argument. It is as if women had an innate tendency to recognize the authority of men.

Do Men Listen?

Even when I read the most violent pamphlets by certain feminist writers, it seems to me that they are fighting more against their own nature than against men, and are furious at not being taken seriously. It is not only men who accuse the women's movement of going to extremes; plenty of women make the same complaint against it. But might it not be that the reason these leaders of Women's Lib. shout so loudly is that they feel that they are not being listened to? It would be an exaggeration to say that women take seriously everything said by men, and that men never take seriously what women say! But we ought at least to recognize that men take what women say less seriously than women take what men say.

That the demand to be taken seriously is a fundamental one for women, was borne in upon me on the occasion of an interview I once gave. It was in fact a young woman, Marie-Claire Lescaze, the daughter of an old friend, who interviewed me. I had at first declined the request for an interview, on the grounds that I had nothing to say beyond what I had already said often enough on the relationships between men and women in marriage and in social life. In the event we had a pleasant lunch together and talked of all sorts of things. When I read her article I saw that she had been able to pick out from our conversation one clear idea, namely that women do not feel that men take them seriously.

The striking thing was the number of people who talked and wrote to me about that interview, saying that in their opinion that was the root of the feminist problem. So I can thank my journalist friend, without whom I should probably never have had the idea of writing this book. She inspired me.

We do not even let women take themselves seriously – we think it would be pretentious on their part. Michèle Perrein, another woman journalist, had an account she had written of an important vice trial turned down. 'I had done something one must not do,' she says, 'I had written it as a woman. Not the sort of woman's article that newspaper editors expect – full of trivialities – but a real woman's article, because I was judging as a woman, in the same way as editors do when they judge as men.' She adds, 'Had I been a man, no doubt my article would have been accepted.'

Benoîte Groult tells of an American experiment which confirms this: 'Two hundred female students were invited to judge a philosophical essay. The first hundred were given an essay signed "John MacKay"; the remaining hundred were given the same essay, but signed "Joan MacKay". John's work, in the vast majority of cases, was found to be original, profound, and imaginative. That of Joan was considered to be superficial, commonplace, and uninteresting.' I really think that it is for that reason that women have written so little until quite recently. They say that they have been reduced to silence by men for centuries. A little exaggerated, perhaps. But what is the good of writing if what one says is considered in advance to be of no significance?

If women feel that they are underestimated, the feminist problem will not be solved simply by giving them rights, political rights, the right to education and a career, to be paid as men are paid, to be heard and to be read. If a woman is not listened to, she will not fully regain confidence in herself, in her own value as a person.

There are lots of married couples where the wife talks, talks at length, and ends up wondering whether her husband is listening at all. 'Sometimes,' one of them tells me, 'I suddenly stop and ask him "Are you listening to me?" Then from behind his newspaper there comes a sort of grunt which at least shows that he has heard the question. But as for an answer to all the problems, often urgent ones, that I am explaining to him, I get none.' Anaïs Nin also speaks of the husband who is 'physically present and mentally absent'.

Women do seem to me to be more courageous than men in facing reality. Even financial reality, when the housewife does not manage to make ends meet in the household budget. At least a couple ought to talk seriously about that, with the figures in front of them. But the husband often avoids that kind of dialogue. He confines himself to saying, 'You'll have to manage with what I give you,' when it is manifestly impossible to keep up the standard of life that he requires with the money that he allows for the housekeeping, and while he is careful to keep no account of what he spends himself.

There are many women who suspect that their husbands are allowing themselves to be swindled by a friend, an associate, or a client, or that their business is going badly, and requires bold measures which they are afraid to take; but they meet only icy silence when they try to broach the subject – even with the most delicate approach: 'What's the matter, dear? You've been so gloomy recently! Are you worried about something? You know I love you, and want to help you.'

There is also the wife who feels that her husband is slipping away from her. He becomes strange, taciturn, or has sudden outbursts of bad temper for no justifiable reason. He keeps from her things that he could very well tell her. Are there other matters which he dare not admit? She would readily forgive him in order to get him back, if there were at least an honest explanation. She takes to spying on him, even though the idea horrifies her. He gets annoyed: 'I've told you, there's nothing the matter. You are imagining things. How tiresome you women are with your fussing!'

The truth is that the other woman is also making a fuss – the woman he has taken up with. She is threatening to commit suicide if he leaves her or betrays her. There are men who allow themselves to remain for a long time in an emotional impasse of this kind, afraid of the emotions on either side of them. They tell stupid and clumsy lies, as if they were unconsciously trying to be caught out! That is often the case: the unconscious seeks the frank confession which fear of emotion denies to the conscious mind.

But why has he formed the attachment to another woman? He will tell his wife when the affair becomes known in spite of him. For a long time he had been disappointed and dissatisfied. And all at once he will heap upon his wife all sorts of complaints which he has never mentioned before – once again for fear of emotion! One can see how this fear secretly poisons a relationship which a little courage could have saved. Or else in order to ward off emotion he puts on an air of pleasantry: 'Several times,' says a woman questioned by Claude Maillard, 'he has talked to me about children: "What about having a baby?" He said it amost with a laugh.'

Women are indeed more courageous in face of life's problems. In my local daily newspaper there is a women's page which carries not only cookery recipes and dress patterns. Every day there are interesting studies on relationships between husband and wife, parents and children, brothers and sisters, family and school, and on the pill, abortion, divorce, social life, the difficulties of a career for women, and the malaise of our civilization.

An analogous page for men has been started, though it appears only once a week. It contains little besides a few trivial jokes of a vaguely sexual or gastronomical nature. Men readily shut their eyes to the things that embarrass them or which might demand personal involvement. They affect to believe that there are only technological problems. They take refuge in the world of things.

Do you not think that the reason why women talk so much is that men hardly ever listen to them? It is a vicious circle: the more silent the man is, the more the woman talks, and the more she talks, the more silent he remains. As a result of having to talk in a void, the woman comes to take her own words less seriously, and her talk turns into aimless chatter. 'Faced with that,' a young wife says, 'you feel you have to talk all the more, to make yourself feel you are bridging the gap and communicating.' There are men who seem to get used to the incessant flow of words, like hearing background music in a restaurant, without ever really listening to it.

A man feels he has to reply to a question put by a man. A woman's question he can leave unanswered. Quite often a woman will go to see a psychotherapist simply in order to be able to talk openly to a man who will actually listen to her. It is enough to change completely the way she talks. She rediscovers her own dignity, and takes herself seriously. 'The psychoanalyst pays attention,' writes Marie Cardinal, 'so you begin yourself to pay attention to what you are saying.' The husband seldom listens like that. Any other man might think she was trying to seduce him, even if he did not himself take the opportunity of doing so.

You may of course think that I am exaggerating when I say that men do not take women seriously, or at least that I am over-generalizing, led astray by the besetting sin of my calling, having seen too many embittered women who think themselves misunder-stood and come to tell me about their imaginary misfortunes. But the problem is so important, it plays, I believe, so great a part in making women feel inferior, that I feel it imperative to explain my point of view.

I have already alluded to it: it can happen, for example, that an intelligent and active woman who is not neurotic and does not doubt her husband's love, will express her disappointment in this way: 'I don't seem able to have a real conversation with my husband.' If I report this remark to the husband, he is astounded, at a loss to understand it. He exclaims with obvious sincerity, 'But we talk about everything! What more does she want?'

No doubt they do talk about everything, but it is all objective, all about facts and ideas, which is what a man is interested in. For a woman real dialogue means talking about her feelings – her own feelings, but even more importantly, about her husband's feelings, which she wants to understand, but which he does not know how to express. In the magazine *Réalités,* Denyse Sergy wrote an admirable 'Open Letter to the Man in My Life'. It is remarkable that such a magazine, devoted as it is to an objective view of things, should publish such a piece. 'I am not your thing,' she writes, 'I am your wife. It is the verb "to share" that I should like to conjugate with you ...' To share, for her, means to share their feelings – and their dialogue is so arid! 'I am like a waterless land, and every day that passes increases my distress.'

We must therefore return to the fundamental distinction which I made at the beginning of this book between the objective, intellectual dialogue, and the emotional, personal dialogue. I return to my own experience, of which I spoke in the first chapter, since I too talked with my wife about everything, and did not see what was missing from our dialogue.

I told you about my friend the Dutch economist, who initiated me into emotional dialogue by talking to me about his life in such a personal fashion that for the first time I was able in my turn to talk about what I had suffered as an orphan. It was he also who initiated me into the practice of meditation. He had talked about it a few days earlier, when I first met him. I can still remember the date – 23 November 1932. It was in the evening, in a fine old house in the Rue Calvin, in Geneva. Three men from Zurich had been speaking there as well: the theologian Emil Brunner, the psychoanalyst Alphonse Maeder, and the writer Théophile Spoerri.

What they said had raised a flood of objections in my mind. But that Dutchman had simply said that his life had been transformed by the practice of regular morning meditation. That got at me, because I had a bad conscience: I knew that my personal spiritual life was too poverty-stricken for one as committed to the church as I was. How was it that that expert, occupying such an important post in the League of Nations, could find the time? I was intrigued. So, at the end of the evening I went straight up to him and asked, 'How long do you spend in meditation in God's presence each morning?' – 'It depends on the day,' he replied; 'usually an hour, sometimes longer.'

The next morning, without making a sound for fear my wife should ask me what I was about, I got up an hour earlier, went into my study and put my watch down in front of me, saying to myself, 'I want to see what happens if I meditate in silence for an hour.' However, the thoughts that kept running through my head were so trivial, so worldly, or so vague, that I could not write them down. I felt that I was on the wrong track. I felt really humiliated. The fact was that I did not know how to listen to God. But as I put my watch back on my wrist I told myself I must persevere for the next few days. Then suddenly a thought came to me: 'Hold on! Perhaps that idea comes from God?' I persevered.

Two weeks later my wife and I made a journey to France, to buy Christmas presents in Lyon. I can still see the cheap little restaurant where we had lunch after our shopping. Nelly said to me, rather hesitantly, 'I should be glad to get back in good time. We set out very early this morning, and I wasn't able to do something I should have liked to do.' – Goodness! Me too! It was the first time I had missed my meditation! We looked at each other and burst out laughing. It was dawning on us that in secret each of us had been conducting an experiment in meditation without daring to talk about it before being sure it was going to work! 'Let's go home, then,' Nelly said, 'and we'll do our meditation together.'

And that is what we did. But I felt even more ill at ease than when I was alone. Actually, I already knew that malaise. We used to experience it every time we had what we used to call a 'little service' together. Nevertheless we were both Christians. It was in fact as Sunday school teachers that we had first met. Our wish had been to make a Christian home; and so, periodically, we decided to hold a 'little service' instead of just saying our prayers in the evening. But how were we to set about it? As Nelly was shy, I took on the job of reading a passage from the Bible and launching into a commentary on it – a sort of mini-sermon! I was playing at being the pastor, while Nelly listened quietly like a well-behaved congregation listening to the minister in church. The awkwardness came from the fact that we both felt it was rather ridiculous.

However, in a meditation I could not get away with it by playing the minister, and we were both quite embarrassed. Then Nelly had a bright idea: 'We'll try again tomorrow,' she said, 'and we can begin by silently asking God what is the cause of the embarrassment.' The next morning I felt as awkward as before. I knew very well that I ought to be relaxed and easy, and simply note down my thoughts. But I was in a complete fog! Nelly, on the other hand, had made the note to which I have already referred, and which I shall never forget: 'You know, you are my doctor, my psychologist, even my pastor, but you are not my husband.'

I was dumbfounded! It was not a complaint on the sexual level. In that sphere we got on well together. No doubt you have understood: Nelly had put her finger unerringly on my essential problem, namely the difficulty that I, like so many men, had in expressing my personal feelings. I was taking refuge in intellectual objectivity, in my role as a doctor, as a psychologist, as a teacher, and even as a theologian. In fact I was taking refuge in the world of things where I felt at ease, because I was not at ease in the world of persons, of personal, emotional commitment either to my wife or to God.

The relationship between the doctor and his patient, between the psychologist and his client, between the teacher and his pupil, between the man who talks and the woman who listens, is an asymmetrical one, to use Eliane Lévy-Valensi's expression. In meditation I had to enter into a symmetrical relationship, in true equality: two equal persons in the presence of God, moved by emotions, feelings, hopes, and fears which they can share on a level of equality. As Françoise Dolto said of Mary of Bethany, Nelly was beginning to come out of her passivity, to become active, to take the lead in a more personal dialogue, and in a way to open for me the communicating door between the world of things and the world of persons.

And so my times of meditation with my wife, which we practised at least once a week until the last day of her life, were for me a long apprenticeship in personal contact, and they also gradually transformed my relationship with my patients. I must, however, recount an incident which occurred many years later. Nelly was reading to me what she had written down in our quiet time, and I started to give her psychological explanations of things she had written. She reacted sharply, thumping the arm of her chair with her fist, and exploding: 'Just you shut up now! It's not your turn to speak! I listened willingly when you read what you had written. Now it's my turn: don't interrupt me. I'm not interested in your psychological interpretations!'

Oh, yes! I often did that, and had not realized the fact. I was distorting the meaning of meditation, giving way to my masculine tendency towards objective analysis. I began to see that there are several ways of listening. You can listen in order to reply, or you can listen simply in order to hear. Listening in order to reply is what we do constantly. Often, in fact, we only half listen, more intent on thinking about our reply, looking out for some remark which will give us the opportunity of a clever answer, of saying what *we* want to say. We are like the hunter waiting with his gun on the edge of the wood for the game to come out. True dialogue means listening not in order to reply, but in order to share in one's partner's emotional life.

13

Contempt

Well, there it is; I can say that I learned gradually to listen better to my wife as well as to other women, to understand them a little, to respect them, to realize our equality as persons, particularly in this search for God's presence, which is more than anything else what makes persons of us. Everything is all right? No more problems? – Alas, no! Such declarations, sincere though they may be, are too simplistic. We have to dig deeper. A recent incident made me acutely aware of this.

My daughter-in-law is an artist, and I like her pictures very much. She is a member of the Society of Women Painters. The Society was organizing an exhibition of self-portraits, and a canvas by my daughter-in-law had been selected. Naturally I congratulated her warmly, and asked her about the opening and closing dates of the exhibition. It was still a long way off, and I thought I should easily find time to go. But when I asked her the dates again, the exhibition had already happened! You can imagine my embarrassment. Here was I, writing this book so that women should be taken seriously. I was caught red-handed failing to do just that!

Monique, my daughter-in-law, said at once, 'If it had been your son exhibiting a picture, I bet you wouldn't have forgotten the date!' She said it kindly, and with a sweet smile, when she might well have made the remark with some bitterness! No, it was rather the teasing tone one uses towards an old man so that he won't take his forgetfulness too much to heart. And I do not think that her remark was an allusion to the ties of blood between me and my son. It had much more to do with the discrimination between the sexes which I am combating in this book. After all, why do women painters have their own Society, if it is not in order to get themselves taken more seriously?

In any case, it was in that sense that I took my daughter-in-law's bantering remark. A lapse of memory is what Freud calls a bungled

104

action, and he has taught us that a bungled action is always the symptom of an inner conflict. It betrays an unconscious feeling – it is the showing of the cloven hoof, one might say. Bungled actions, together with dreams, are the best means of exploring the unconscious and seeking out the feelings which we have repressed into it.

The incident, therefore, at once struck me as a most humiliating revelation for me. Here I was, putting all my conscious sincerity into the writing of this book, and all the time in the obscure depths of my mind there lurked an unconscious contempt for women! That means that all the zeal I bring to this affirmation of the fundamental equality between women and men, I can look upon as a conscious compensation for an unconscious contempt. Naturally, I find the diagnosis hard to take. Does it really mean that I too despise women, in the depths of my unconscious mind? I protest as I did when a woman psychoanalyst told me recently that I have an unconscious fear of women!

Have I any justification at all for being so surprised? The unconscious is like the geologists' fossils: the deposit of the past, both our own personal past and that of the human race. We all undergo social conditioning. It really would be arrogant of me to suppose that I alone had escaped its effects! The last four centuries have been filled with contempt for women. I may of course consciously react against such a widespread prejudice, but how can I avoid some vestige of it remaining in my subconscious? And if that is the case with me, it is the same for every other man. That in all probability lies at the root of the whole feminist problem.

Obviously, then, it is not to be resolved simply by granting civil and political rights to women, not even by appointing a woman prime minister, as has just happened in Great Britain as I write. The problem lies deeper. It is a psychological one. If there persists in the depths of the masculine psyche a repressed contempt for women, the applause, the congratulations and tributes addressed to Mrs Thatcher on her election are, like all the gallantries ever addressed to women, a veneer, polished but deceptive.

Of course it was necessary first to attack institutions, to give women the rights which have been unjustly withheld from them; but that is not enough. The point is made, for example, by Michèle Perrein. She acknowledges the progress made, to which the nomination of women to high political office bears witness, but she adds, 'That does not mean that contempt for the female sex has died away.' It is important, therefore, to recognize the psychological problem for what it is – much more deepseated than all our arguments about the role of women, and much more difficult to solve. Because Freud has taught us that we cannot eradicate an unconscious impulse unless we first become aware of its existence. And because Jung has taught us that in the collective make-up of the human race the unconscious factors are invincible, and will always win against even the most generous conscious aspirations.

Last week I was giving a talk in one of the many seminars on preparation for retirement at which I am called upon to speak. Mlle Jacqueline Golay, a dietician from Lausanne, was to give a talk before mine, and I went early in order to hear her. It was in a lovely spot, overlooking the Lake of Geneva. We had time for a chat over coffee before the session began. She asked me about this book I am writing. 'Well,' I said, 'I think that there is in men's hearts a certain unconscious contempt for women ...' I could not finish my sentence – it was she who finished it for me: '... Yes, a contempt which women certainly feel!'

So here was a woman who was highly trained, doing an important scientific job which she loves, enjoying considerable public respect, and like me giving lectures – very active also in the Consumers' Federation, which devotes itself to the unmasking of commercial practices prejudicial to housewives – and who suddenly tells me that women feel this unconscious contempt on the part of men! She was looking me in the eye, with a mischievous expression in her own. I could see that she was thinking, 'If only men would at least admit it, instead of denying it!'

Yes, I do believe that women can read the unconscious mind better than men. Men, of course, are not incapable of doing so, witness Freud himself, who nevertheless felt himself to be, as we have seen, 'so very masculine'. But for that they need a whole technological apparatus, a whole system of interpretation. Women, on the other hand, often have a direct intuition as to a man's repressed feelings. This is a source of misunderstandings between spouses, when the husband protests that his wife is 'imagining things'.

That contempt for the female sex is quite conscious, openly flaunted even, in many men, nobody will deny. Gisèle Halimi tells of how upset her father was when she was born, in Tunisia, because it was a girl. In fact she turned out to be very bright at school, whereas her brother was a dunce. But her father cared only about the brother. It often happens like that. Obviously her father's contempt for her was the source of Gisèle Halimi's feminist vocation. Throughout her youth she worked hard. She sought in books, as she puts it, 'the means to be free'; and she chose to be a barrister in order to be able to defend 'Italians, Tunisians, Arabs under colonial rule ... and women'. She goes on to tell of how for her first case in court she arranged her hair and everything else so as to make herself look plain: 'In order to make them forget that I was a woman,' she writes. 'To make them listen to me. To make them take me seriously.' A strange paradox – her life has become an exciting adventure, whereas it would have been much more ordinary if her father had cherished her!

Obviously I should have no difficulty in gleaning from feminist literature further instances of the quite conscious and cynical contempt with which man can treat woman. One of the most trenchant examples is Kate Millett's book *Sexual Politics*. It opens with a passage from Henry Miller's *Sexus*, an atrocious sexual scene in which his hero is maltreating Ida with a savagery that is as refined as it is brutish, exclaiming afterwards, 'I did it expressly to annoy and humiliate her.' And further on: 'I just didn't give a damn for her, as a person.'

I have to admit that I was irritated by Kate Millett. The tone of her book, too, is extreme. I felt humiliated to think that I also was a man, and tried to assure myself that I was not like all those men of whose shocking attitudes she complains. It was the incident of my daughter-in-law's exhibition which forced me to recognize that I was then in exactly the same state of mind as the Pharisee in Jesus' well-known parable, who prayed thus: 'I thank you, God, that I am not as other men are' (Luke 18.11).

This is an appropriate point to recall the remark by the psychoanalyst Dr Aloys von Orelli: 'We are irritated by that in others which we have repressed in ourselves.' Indeed, there is close agreement on this point between ancient gospel and modern psychology. The sin which Jesus constantly denounces is not so much that of brutish men, but that of decent people who in fact look down with contempt on others from the height of their own good consciences. It is also our hypocrisy that psychological analysis constantly reveals. Women suffer at the hands of the brutes, of course, but they also suffer in a more confused sort of way from the unconscious contempt they see in all of us men. What really highlights the feminist problem is the fact that a cultured woman like Annie Leclerc, a professor of philosophy, and manifestly a kindly person, is able to write, 'We are despised'; and in doing so she is thinking not of a few exceptions, but of the attitude of men in general.

I am prepared to concede that the word 'contempt' is rather strong. We ought to speak of 'disdain'. But perhaps even the shade of difference in meaning between the two words hides our need to justify ourselves. I speak of contempt because those whom we treat with disdain feel it as contempt. All the victims of the various kinds of racism feel this, and what we are dealing with here is a kind of racism. Contempt is the social problem *par excellence.* It is those who are despised who are conscious of this contempt. Those who despise them do so without realizing it. Among the victims of this social contempt are Marx's proletarians, coloured people, social misfits, failures, the mentally ill, the aged, victimized ethnic minorities, those on the left in the eyes of those on the right and *vice versa*, even unbelievers in the eyes of believers, or believers in the eyes of unbelievers.

How many conflicts there are which have as their fundamental cause this feeling of being despised! You know how poisoned a marital conflict can become when one of the partners feels despised by the other. It is complicated by the fact that contempt is often mutual: contempt answers contempt. Jacques Ellul points out the hypocrisy involved when we despise a country for being racist, since there is racism, open or hidden to varying degrees, in every country and in the hearts of all of us.

It was contempt of men that I found in Kate Millett's book as I read it. The poor despise the rich, too, even though the social esteem enjoyed by the rich protects them from feeling it. The same thing happens between man and woman. Kate Millett may irritate me, but she does not hurt me; whereas the contempt, even if unconscious, which a woman senses in a man gives her a feeling of inferiority which prevents her from realizing her full potential.

You know how boys will indulge in rough behaviour and fight each other, even if they do not wish to, for fear of being thought sissy, or 'chicken'. When I was at school it was called *cognance* (lit. 'bashing'). It was usually a strong boy who had challenged a weaker one, who did not dare to run away. The cry 'Cognance!' would go up, and we would all run to watch the spectacle. But it was nearly always disappointing, because the real motive of the heroes was not the fighting, but to cut a figure in the eyes of the other boys, so the fight was soon over.

Boys make fun of girls, especially on the approach of adoles-

cence, when desire is awakening, though it is not yet ready to
express itself openly, and so it is hidden under sarcastic remarks.
An attractive woman may doubt her seductive powers all her life
because a brother was once in the habit of referring to her as an ugly
duckling, so that she never discovers the make-up or the hair-style
that suits her, and even thinks that men are looking at her with contempt when their glances are in fact prompted by desire. Another
imposes a fiendishly strict diet upon herself in order to slim, simply
because her brother used to call her 'Fatty'.

Christianity proclaims that the despised are blessed. Buddhism
proclaims the same, as did the prophets of Israel; and so do all
religions, even Islam, which nevertheless professes contempt for
women. But to spread this message they seek out the most brilliant
pastors, the most gifted priests, the most prestigious ayatollahs. I
felt this acutely when I was working in the church – that pride of
place was accorded to intellectual capacity and oratorical talent,
while pastors who lacked these qualities were little thought of – and
were made to feel their incapacity! It was to one of the latter that I
went to ask forgiveness when I realized that the person was more
important than the personage, as I told you at the end of Chapter 1.

Despite all the sermons from priests and pastors society remains
full of prejudices, and the one about male superiority persists
despite all the concessions made to feminism. Women themselves
more often than not believe themselves to be inferior, as I have had
occasion to observe. There I am in agreement with Kate Millett,
who writes that they 'despise both themselves and each other'.
Our society, like our own hearts, puts the masculine values first:
strength, success, prestige. We sing of love among men, but go on
competing against each other, trying to outshine each other, to
triumph over each other. And in order to get themselves accepted as
equals women have to play the same dangerous game. In my lonely
childhood I dreamed often enough of being a great general or a
great statesman – more even than being a great doctor – and of
course of being a model of humility at the same time!

Then there is the intellectual prejudice which values the head
more highly than the heart, objective knowledge above feeling.
Now, I can see well enough that during the early years of my
marriage I considered myself superior to my wife because I was
better educated. If anyone had suggested to me that I looked down
upon her I should have violently denied it! And I think that she too
considered herself inferior, and set me on a pedestal, as so many

wives do. I could see that she suffered from feelings of inferiority, but the very efforts I made to explain this to her and to exhort her to have more confidence in herself put me above her, because I was dictating to her what to do! It was not until we came together in God's presence, and I confessed my own feelings, that she felt that I needed her help as much as she needed mine, and that I had as much to learn from her as she from me. That is real equality.

Every living being needs to be valued and respected. I think it is this need which has mobilized women in the feminist movement. In order to be appreciated like men they have sought to work like men, study like men, take part in politics like men, and often to behave like them. That is why they turn themselves into servants, although they complain about it, why they allow themselves to be so easily exploited. It is even why they sometimes give in to the sexual desire of a man without love, which is against their nature. And so one realizes that all this is not enough. Many working women, particularly single women, have said to me, 'The service I give is appreciated, but not my person – I am just an instrument of work.' Women, precisely because they have a keener sense of the person than men have, also need, more than men do, to feel that they are recognized as persons.

From where, then, does the contempt of man for woman come – this contempt that is so difficult to eradicate, consciously expressed in brutes and bullies (who will not be reading this book), unconscious in large numbers of others who are full of good will and honestly desirous of equality? Although, as we have seen, the social condition of women deteriorated rapidly from the Renaissance up to the end of the last century, there is no doubt that this psychological problem of masculine disdain goes back to earliest times. It has been claimed that long ago there were matriarchal societies. But Françoise Héritier assures us that 'they have never existed'.

It has been suggested that there was a time when a change of climate drove man from the forests, where food was plentiful, into the savannas, where he had to hunt game and cut flints to make weapons. Marie Cardinal imagines that he would have said then to his wife, 'You have a child in your womb, another at your breast, and a third on your knee; you can't come hunting with me; gather some bilberries while I am away.' He would thus have given her to understand that he looked upon hunting as a more noble adventure than picking bilberries.

It seems unlikely. For while she was gathering the bilberries she was making children, and we know that the desire to have descendants was much greater in primitive man than today. The worst curse, for a woman, was to be barren. The supreme reward promised by Yahweh to Abraham is to have offspring as numerous as the grains of sand on the seashore (Gen. 22.17). What the geneticists call parental investment was without doubt, even for the father, higher in the beginning than it is now. Today man is a builder; he aspires to leave behind him a work, and not only a line of descendants.

Annie Leclerc has a passage in which she mischievously imagines that man, in the distant past when he did not yet understand his role in procreation, might have been jealous of woman, who was capable of producing children: 'Why her, and not me?' Whereupon man got his own back by denigrating woman. But that, she adds sententiously, was to his own detriment, because 'vengeful man could not be happy'. However, she relents and admits that it was also to get her own revenge that she permitted herself such a fantasy!

A fantasy? Yes, but one which I think does have a grain of truth in it. Modern psychology has clearly shown that man does not act in accordance with objective reason, but is guided by his feelings, and especially by that incredible mixture of contradictory feelings that arise from his sexuality: desires, fears, reciprocal jealousies, envies, revulsions, loves and hates, veneration and contempt, spite, and the impulse to possess. All these feelings are linked, and call to one another, like dancers in an endless round.

To say that it is through pride that man has tried to dominate woman explains nothing, because women are as proud as men. To say that it is because he is the stronger does not explain why he uses his strength in that way. It is the feelings which mobilize strength. The poets had already said so. Aesop, that witty little Greek slave, had written his fable of the fox and the grapes: being unable to reach the fine grapes because they were too high up, the fox goes off saying that they are not ripe. Contempt, then, is bound up with frustrated desire. And woman, the eternal temptress, is eternally despised.

Desire comes into play in every department of our social life. I remember one day – it was in the days when one still gave a tip to the waitress in a café – when I realized that I gave a bigger tip when the waitress was pretty, wearing a short skirt or a daringly low-cut dress. Basically, I was paying for the spectacle. The girl was pleased, even if she was too polite to show it. But in doing so I was treating her as a thing and not with the respect she merited as a person. I see now that in that act my unconscious, repressed contempt for women was showing its cloven hoof. In feminist books the writer often says how exasperated she is by the lustful glances of men, and it is no doubt because she feels that they are a sign of contempt.

While contempt is related to desire, it is also allied to fear: all men are afraid of women – it is the fear of the unknown, for there is so much in the nature of women that seems mysterious to men. In this they are like all male animals, afraid of the female they are courting. If you doubt this, read a book like that by Vitus B. Dröscher: 'They love and kill ... like men.' I too was astonished to discover that throughout almost the whole of the animal kingdom the males have a terrible fear of the females. It is amusing to read of the ruses, the cheating, the stratagems, the disguises, and the wiles to which they have to resort in order to perform their conjugal duty.

What is it that these poor males are afraid of? In some cases, of course, it is of being eaten, and they quickly make off after fertilizing the female! But in the majority it is the fear of failure, of being repulsed and rejected. It would be surprising if man were the only species to whom the rule did not apply. In fact it is easy to see that all men are afraid of all women, no less, if not more, than all women are afraid of all men. How contradictory human nature is! Pride and shame, desire and fear, courage and cowardice, confidence and mistrust, constantly coexist in all our hearts, and even lend each other their dynamism.

Even animals, however, have this fear of being repulsed. Dröscher tells the touching story of the poor male who must first construct a nice little house into which to invite his beloved, in the hope of being accepted if the house pleases her. The case is confirmed by another zoologist, Richard Dawkins, in his book *The Selfish Gene*. He explains its mechanism in accordance with the latest genetic theory, the so-called 'social theory founded on natural selection'.

We know that the fundamental principle of the theory of genes is that natural selection favours those behaviour patterns which ensure the greatest chances of survival for the genes transmitted to the descendants. This survival is more probable if the father is faithful, if he remains with the mother and helps in the nurture of the offspring. If not, he is no more than an adventurer, a philanderer who does not contribute his share of the 'parental investment'. In this connection Dawkins uses the term which so often comes from the pens of the feminists – exploitation. 'What can the female do to fight against the exploitation of the male?' Well, she puts the male through a veritable fidelity test during his courtship, by resisting his advances over a long period: if he spends the time constructing a nest – a family home, that is – there is some chance that he will make a faithful husband and a devoted father.

Thus, when a girl repels a boy's first advances, when she says no but thinks yes, as the saying is, that has nothing to do with feminine duplicity, either mysterious or diabolical. It is simply that she is programmed that way by her genetic code. And the man who shows off in front of a woman, particularly when he emulates Don Juan and boasts of his conquests, was paralysed by unbelievable shyness when he confessed his first love! How many subtleties there are in all this, and how many masterpieces literature has fashioned from them!

14

What Genetics has to Say

I found Richard Dawkins' book really exciting. It is wonderful, is it not, to be so enthusiastic at the age of eighty-one! I should like now to share my excitement. Actually it is the same enthusiasm as I felt in my youth when I read J.H. Fabre's *Souvenirs entomologiques*. Later, there was Adolf Portmann, the Basle zoologist: if you want to understand humans, he used to say, there's nothing like observing the habits and customs of animals, so diverse, so subtle, so effective, and often so enigmatic.

In order to explain what man is, Richard Dawkins begins with an account of Darwin's theory of natural selection, followed by that of the Dutch botanist Hugo de Vries, who showed that evolution does not proceed continuously but by successive mutations. He then turns to how these doctrines have been illuminated by Mendel's work in genetics, rediscovered after the neglect of more than a century; and finally to the theory of genes of the Danish scientist Johanson, universally accepted now by scientists, the importance of which is obvious to all. Genes are the 'atoms of heredity'. All this is well known, and is to be found set out with remarkable clarity in such books as those by Jacques Monod and François Jacob.

Now, genes do not transmit, as Darwin had seen, only the morphological and functional characteristics which differentiate species (anatomy and physiology), but also their characteristic behaviour, which is the subject of ethology, the science of behaviour, about which Dawkins writes. The same laws of natural selection apply to both.

As you know it is a question of chemistry: the nucleic acid in the chromosomes of each cell in the organism is disposed in extremely long chains twisted into double spirals, and grouped into 'large molecules', called DNA. These chains might be likened to immense rings of dancers, in which the participants, of four different kinds, disposed in a different order in each ring, hold each other by the

114

hand. This is the genetic code. As in data-processing it forms a coded message which cannot do anything of itself, but which controls the proteins. These cannot act by themselves, but only on command: real team-work! And from two points of view: what are 'proteins for the chemists' are 'genes for the geneticists'.

In fact these four kinds of dancers are like four letters of an alphabet, and just as letters take on meaning when they are assembled into words, they too form a message. This message will be transmitted, half from one parent and half from the other, to their descendants through the sex cells, but previous to that it is transmitted by copying from cell to cell throughout the organism. So that every cell contains, to use Dawkins' analogy, 'the architect's plans for the entire building' together with 'instructions for use', and this process takes place 'six thousand million million million times' in a human body!

Each actual copy is short-lived, whether in an organism or in those of its descendants. It is the interminable series of copies which lasts. So the essential characteristic of the gene is this ability to reproduce itself by means of successive copies. The genes are therefore called 'replicators'. Their sole law seems to be to ensure their survival as far as possible, and the organism is only a 'survival machine' for them, and sex a device for making possible their survival from generation to generation.

This is where natural selection comes in: in every operation involving a long series of copies, errors can occur. Some may increase the chances of survival, others compromise them. Selection will reward the former by incorporating them into the reproductive series, and penalize the latter by extinguishing them. Note that in all this there is no question of instinct. Here is a book devoted entirely to animal behaviour and to the relationship between the sexes, and there is no mention of the word, which was so frequent in the scientific works of my youth! Similarly there is no longer any mention of determinism: only of programming.

The analogy with cybernetics is in fact striking. Everything to do with our life and our death is programmed by our genes, even down to the minutest details, including each of our cells and every facet of our behaviour. It seems that Jesus had an inkling of this when he said, 'Every hair on your head has been counted' (Matt. 10.30). But consider – when a computer is constucted and programmed, it is with a fixed end in view: the notion of programming has an inescapable flavour of purpose; but in my young days there was no worse heresy in science than to propose a solution implying purpose. How things have changed! Even more suggestive of purpose is J. Maynard Smith's ESS theory, of which Dawkins writes: 'I have a hunch that we may come to look back on the invention of the ESS concept as one of the most important advances in evolutionary theory since Darwin.' Now let us note that the letters ESS stand for 'Evolutionarily Stable Strategy'.

Strategy! What more purposive word could you have than that? Can you imagine a strategy without a strategist who draws it up, since it is nothing other than a set of manoeuvres which he chooses in order to achieve his purpose? Jacques Monod, to avoid the word 'purpose', says it in Greek, and speaks of 'teleonomy'. It is no good Dawkins telling us that it is a metaphor, and that 'we are not talking about conscious strategies, but about unconscious behaviour programs laid down by genes', he cannot avoid the implication of purpose in the word itself. Such an interpretation had in any case already been introduced by Darwin, and the Nobel prize-winner François Jacob in his authoritative history of genetics says bluntly, 'Natural selection imposes finality.'

Of course I am not complaining about that. I am simply noting that the passionate controversies of my youth, between the causal determinism of science and the finalism of faith in a creator God who rules the world, have long since been overtaken. They had already been overtaken by psychology, if not by that of Freud, who saw only blind impulses, at least by that of Jung, whose archetypes are like harbour lights towards which the navigator sails. What the biologists are suggesting is basically an automatic finalism, the result of the blind interplay of natural phenomena. Of course, God remains invisible still! Are not the heavenly bodies in their orbits obeying an automatic finalism?

So I willingly accept the ESS theory, particularly as I at once saw the use I could make of it here in support of my thesis, as I shall presently show. What then is this theory of 'evolutionarily stable strategy'? – Here, in outline, is one of the simplest of Dawkins' illustrations of it. There are species of birds which on average incubate one egg at a time, others incubate two, and others three, and so on. In his terms he therefore speaks of a 'gene for laying one egg', a 'gene for laying two eggs', and so on. What is it that in a given species causes one of these genes to dominate and be transmitted rather than the other? Is not the chance of survival of the genes the better, the greater the number of eggs in the clutch? – No, he says, because 'increased bearing is bound to be paid for in less efficient caring'. And this caring is no trivial matter: 'a parent great tit brings an average of one item of food to the nest every 30 seconds of daylight'.

There is therefore an optimum number of offspring. If there are too many, they will not be adequately fed. Without sufficient food the young birds die within a few hours and the parents will end up with less offspring than those parents which have incubated 'just the right number'. This 'strategy' of too many eggs, which one could term 'inflationary', is therefore bound to fail; it is not 'stable'.

We have here the model of a process which obtains throughout the whole field of biology – regulation on constant averages. For example, our body temperature of 37°C, or the fixed ratio of salt, sugar, urea, hormones, or any other substance in our blood and tissues. Much study has been made of the mechanisms by which deviations from the norm are constantly corrected. These mechanisms are evidently controlled by the genes, and transmitted from generation to generation by replication.

Now, however, we are concerned with a quite different question: not, for example, how the correction of the temperature on the average of 37° is brought about, but why the constant average is 37°, and not 27° or 47°. It is the same problem as the number of eggs in a clutch; and here again it is natural selection and ESS which choose (if one may use the term) the constant average.

I can think of another example: the duration of pregnancy is about nine months in the human species, with some oscillations in the case of premature babies, and births which are delayed so long that they have to be induced. But why nine months? There must be genes for nine months, just as there were genes for three eggs. The explanation is no doubt similar: genes for less than nine months would produce premature infants who would die; genes for more than nine months, infants so large that both they and the mothers would die. Neither the one nor the other would thus have any opportunity of transmitting themselves to their descendants. It is always the survival of the genes which ensures their success by selection.

Here I ought to mention a controversy between scientists which is of great importance to our author. He maintains, with David Lack and others, that it is only the opportunity for survival of the gene which controls selection, whence the title of his book – *The Selfish Gene*, whereas Darwin, and others such as Wynne-Edwards, in-

117

voked 'the good of the species'. Thus, in the case of the eggs, it would be possible to maintain that if the clutch consisted of a greater number of eggs, the population would become too numerous for the available territory and the species would die of famine. Thus there must be 'altruistic' genes which would sacrifice themselves for the species, like a soldier giving his life for his country in a war.

I am not qualified to judge between these two theories, but I incline towards that of Richard Dawkins, for my whole career has convinced me of the universal natural selfishness of men, whose victims were my care. My Calvinist theology also turns me in that direction. Throughout my childhood I heard the liturgical prayer: 'Incapable of ourselves of doing any good, we humbly beg you to aid us in our misery.' In these days of the glorification of man, there are pastors who no longer dare say that prayer. It is amusing now to see the biologists taking over, and affirming that our all-powerful genes programme us exclusively to be selfish! For altruism Dawkins relies only on education, while I rely on the grace of God.

This controversy aside, it is clear that natural selection operates only in the long term, since it works through successive replication of genes from generation to generation. Consequently the author introduces an important distinction which I shall use presently in the analysis of the crisis of our civilization and of the mission of women in the world: the distinction between short-term and long-term benefits.

Thus he has a lot to say about 'cheats'. It is a surprising term, because it usually has a moral sense, whereas with Dawkins it signifies, basically, the nonconformists, those who do not behave in accordance with the norm. This happens for example in the case of mutual grooming, which plays an important and more or less ritualized social and hygienic role amongst certain animals. The 'cheat' is an individual who allows himself to be groomed by another in parts of his body which he himself cannot reach, but who refuses to groom the other in return. The matter is in fact more complicated, because there are also the 'grudgers', who refuse to groom those who have refused to groom them. By means of complicated calculations for which he had to use a computer, the author shows that the cheat wins only a short-term advantage, not a long-term one. But this is not difficult to understand, since his advantage is that by cheating he will reproduce himself more than the rest. However, it is obvious that as the number of cheats increases, the benefits of cheating will diminish, until in a population entirely composed of cheats, no one wins. Cheating pays only in the short term. One is reminded of the 'delays of divine justice' of which Plutarch wrote.

This business of cheating is intensely interesting. I had already been struck, from my reading of other ethologists such as Dröscher, by the fact that the animal world abounds in ruses, camouflage, and trickery, just like the world of men. All animal mimicry, often quite astonishing in its artfulness, is cheating. There is the intriguing case of Trivers' little 'cleaner-fish', which larger fish are careful not to eat, because they serve the larger fish by swimming into their mouths to clean their teeth for them. These cleaner-fish are distinguished by having 'special stripy patterns' and peculiar dancing displays. Other fish, however, imitate their stripes and their dances so well that they too escape being eaten!

The cleaner-fish remind me of my home help who comes in on a Saturday morning to tidy up all the things that I have left scattered about during the week, and who tells me that she likes doing it. That reminds me that it is time to extrapolate these zoological thoughts into the field of our civilization and of the problem of women. Richard Dawkins himself invites us to do so when he asserts that in human societies the history of cultures has taken over from the evolution of the species, and that it obeys the same laws. These views are reminiscent of those of Teilhard de Chardin, with his noosphere succeeding the biosphere. Jacques Monod also invites us to think along these lines, despite his opposition to Teilhard de Chardin, since he writes that with the appearance of man a new world was born, 'the world of ideas; and a new evolution, the evolution of culture, became possible'.

Dawkins shows that it is also by means of 'replicators', by means of innumerable copies transmitted from generation to generation, that cultural norms are fixed. He even invents a word, based on a Greek root, the 'meme' (he wanted it to sound something like gene). But we may speak more simply of ideas – the word Jacques Monod used. Socrates has been dead for a long time, but his idea 'Know thyself' has been faithfully copied from brain to brain throughout history, to come into my own brain.

Another example is a musical idea from a Beethoven symphony which I can hum. Similarly Jesus' exhortation 'Love one another' has been copied down the ages, and has prompted innumerable initiatives of love in a human race programmed by nature for selfishness. In the same way the idea of the radical inferiority of women, proclaimed at the time of the Renaissance – it was a mutation! – has been copied again and again through four centuries, and there remains a vestige of it in my own unconscious, as I have had to recognize.

You will remember that I pointed out that the Renaissance made a choice: it was a 'strategy'. I understand why Richard Dawkins' book had such an effect on me: it provided me with the key word I was looking for in support of the thesis which I am maintaining here in my book. I can employ the same word 'strategy', because Dawkins tells us that the strategy of ideas plays the same role in the evolution of culture as the strategy of the genes in the evolution of species. Only, where the impulse of the genes was 'unconscious and blind', that of ideas is imbued with conscious foresight.

So what did happen at the time of the Renaissance? As we have seen, in the awful chaos and despair of that time, as described by Delumeau, men chose a strategy – a masculine strategy. They enthroned, one might say, all the masculine values – power, combativeness, rational thought, cold objective relationships, technology, the manipulation of things – and Roman law which sanctioned the dominance of the male, who was better fitted for the exercise of these virile virtues. From then on, man has experienced, in Vergote's words, 'the secret fear of giving himself up to phantasmagoria'. And so he represses the feminine values – feeling, sensibility, an understanding heart, intuition, personal relationship, and mysticism. At the same time woman, the incarnation of this repudiated aspect of human nature, was relegated to the strict limits of the home, away from the conduct of affairs.

All this is implied in the saying of Descartes, 'I think, therefore I am', in which man defines himself in terms of himself alone, without reference to others. It is implied above all in his intention of devising a rigorous method of banishing doubt and of building, stone by stone, a scientific civilization. Since then Nature has been no more than an object, an object of study and exploration; and woman an instrument in the service of men in their great enterprise, to comfort them in their moments of repose and to satisfy their sex instinct. Even in sex priority has been given to its masculine aspect – desire, lust – over its feminine aspect – tenderness and personal relationship.

One can understand and even admire what happened at the time of this cultural mutation at the Renaissance. At a time of extreme distress, as for instance when shipwreck threatens, there is no time to spare for the queasy or the tender-hearted; what is required is action, and reliable and effective support. That is what objective science seemed to offer. It was a strategy, that is to say a coherent and logical set of bold measures, to overcome a tragic fate. Galileo, Copernicus, Bacon, Descartes, and many others, opened breaches in the enemy front of the obscure mysteries of Nature. At last it was going to be possible to acquire reliable and objective knowledge as a defence against all the ills that flesh was heir to.

They were followed by an army of researchers and men of action who threw themselves into the breaches, enlarging them in every direction, and winning victory after victory. It was the great epic of science, which was providing rational explanations for everything that had not been understood, and of technology, which was finding solutions to every problem. There was also the saga of the exploration of the planet, and of colonization, in which natives were treated as women had been treated, as mute servants of the masters in their great work, from which, in any case, they benefited through the prosperity which it brought.

As you know, this virile strategy produced results. Never mind the women and their sensibilities – debate about the strategy was confined to men, who are fond of grand theories, and do not bother themselves with either details or feelings. The strategy was so successful that it fostered new acts of faith and new hopes: that one day everything would be known and understood through science; and that all the difficulties of life could be reduced to problems of technique; later came the idea of controlling history instead of being controlled by it, and of solving economic and social problems through dialectic; then the solution of the problems of psychological forces by the analysis of impulses; and finally the annexation of the moon and space to man's terrestrial empire which had become too small for him.

The strategy paid off. Man wanted power and he has obtained it. His power has been multiplied not just ten or a hundred times, but by millions, with the atomic bomb. But how quickly the bomb has become a burden to him! Its only use is to prevent the explosion of another one. That is a mercy so far as it goes, but it has its tragic side. It is the bomb which confirms our feeling that there are limits to the great saga, limits that are inherent in the laws of Nature itself.

Let us return, then, to Richard Dawkins and his ESS. In genetics and ethology the whole argument is based on a study of the long-term effects and repercussions of a mutation. It is stable only if these effects are of long-term benefit to it, and do not compromise it by modifying the conditions in which the mutation occurred and which favoured the strategy it adopted. The strategy of the Renaissance has paid dividends in the short term – for four centuries, in fact – but in the long term it will not do so, and there is a general feeling that we are approaching the end of the short-term benefits.

We are now facing the problem of Dawkins' 'cheats', who have the advantage only so long as they are the first few of their kind, but lose it when their numbers increase. This was the case with the first to possess the atomic bomb. It was also the case with the first to consume energy on a lavish scale, that is to say those who first profited from the mutation we call industrialization. Now that other countries have imitated them, however, we have an energy crisis. It is important to see that the prosperity of the West has been made possible only because it involved only a minority of the human race.

Thus the very success of a mutation may bring in its train long-term disasters, because the movement started at the time of a mutation carries on inexorably, developing, increasing in breadth and speed. Philippe Mottu has shown this to be true of the acceleration in technological progress: 'Fifty-six years elapsed between the invention of the telephone and its practical application, thirty-five years in the case of radio, fifteen for radar, twelve for television. But it took only seven years to go from nuclear fission to the terrible reality of Hiroshima, five years for transistors to go from the laboratory into the shops, and only three years for the laser beam, the latest brain-child of modern technology.' We all feel caught in this historical movement, which is beginning to seem like a nightmare race to disaster. Some strategies are 'evolutionarily stable' (the ESS), others are not.

The strategy of the Renaissance is unstable in the long run. It has produced a marvellous firework display of scientific and technological progress. But it is like an engine that has started racing and cannot be stopped. A new distress is gripping us – the fear of a civilization devoid of all humanity, in which the person is stifled by things. Why is it that this strategy cannot be stable in the long term? Because it has thrust aside one half of the human race; it has deprived our civilization of the gifts that only women could bring to it. In doing so it has discarded one whole aspect of human life – the emotional and non-rational side of our nature, and our need for

122

personal relationship. What is more, this is the more important half of life, since, as psychology has taught us, man is not guided by reason but by his emotions.

15

The Mission of Women in the World

Now, in this twentieth century of ours, a new mutation is appearing: the liberation of women from the ghetto in which they have been confined. This liberation has of course not yet been completed, but it is far enough advanced to be considered as one of the most important events in the evolution of civilization at the present time. There is one other, namely decolonization, and I have already pointed out the close connection between these two movements – the fact that they are both part of a great struggle by the despised to be recognized fully as persons.

Will this be a 'stable' mutation, in Dawkins' terms? Or rather, by correcting the error of the Renaissance, will it allow Western civilization to become stable, to continue to develop harmoniously, instead of rushing into catastrophe? It is obvious that something has got to change! Can we look for that change coming from the influence of women, as they assume an increasingly important role in society? If not, all the feminist movement will have achieved will be the incorporation of women into the masculine system set up at the time of the Renaissance.

As we have seen, towards the end of the Middle Ages women were beginning to emerge from the inferior status they had had from ancient times. Then, in the great panic of the Renaissance, the brake was put on hard with the return to Roman law, to the domination of man over woman, and the triumph of the masculine ideal of objectivity and power. Now, women have begun to win back their rights. It seems to me that that confers upon them an obligation, a mission to change the direction of the evolution of our civilization so as to make it more stable.

I warn you, ladies, that it will not be easy, because men have become accustomed over four centuries to making all the decisions. They are willing now to let you have a hand in their affairs, provided you stay quiet. A man does not like to receive advice from a woman, whoever she is – even if she is the woman who shares with him the responsibility of his life. I have experienced this time and time again. When my wife expressed an opinion different from mine, my first reaction was generally to think that she was wrong and I was right. All the arguments to demonstrate this came at once into my mind.

Only afterwards, thinking it over, and often in my meditation, did the thought occur to me that I might examine more calmly whether she might be right; and even whether what she was saying might be a warning from God. Then, however, the demon of my masculine vanity raised its ugly head, and I reflected that God could well have spoken to me direct, rather than through Nelly.

That reminds me of an incident which took place in Holland. It was at a meeting of doctors presided over by Professor Van den Speck. Suddenly he said, 'We should also like to hear what Mme Tournier has to say', and he called her to the rostrum. I especially remember one thing she said: 'I learnt that when I had something important to say to my husband, I had to be careful to choose the right moment and the right tone of voice.' All my colleagues laughed: we always laugh when the speaker utters a truth that we usually conceal. For my part, I was astonished – I, who thought myself so attentive and so ready to listen!

I am not the only one who makes that mistake. The truth is that men have run on their own for centuries, as fast as they have been able. They are so fond of showing off their prowess and their technical skill! They wanted to achieve a 4% growth per annum. They ought to have known what that comes to at the end of four centuries – they are keen enough on figures. It can only lead to excess. I realized that when reading Jacques Ellul's last book, *The Betrayal of the West*. At first I was surprised that he said that it was Reason which had been betrayed, when it was he who long before me had denounced modern rationalism and the ascendancy of technology.

I soon saw, however, that the Reason of which he is speaking there is not that of rationalism, which denies the knowledge of the heart, but the Reason which is the opposite of unreason and of excess. It was a woman, a virgin, who had taught man wisdom and moderation. Her temple on the Acropolis was large and imposing, but by no means 'hyper-super-extra'. On the contrary, it was the symbol of balance, of harmony, of the moderation which characterized that golden age.

It was a woman too who invited man to know himself. In modern times, however, he has preferred to know the world, the object rather than the subject. It has taken him as far as the moon. I am in no way denigrating that achievement: I look upon it as magnificent. It only needed the sense of the person to be given as much attention as the technology of things, the feminine principle as much as the masculine. As they regain their proper place in society, therefore, is it not the mission of women to demand not only justice for themselves, but also a just moderation in civilization?

Many young people are demanding it, not only in words, but also by their violent reactions, their challenging behaviour. I have just been reading a marvellous book by a Catholic priest, Fr Stan Rougier, who has worked for many years among young delinquents. He quotes a large number of letters and declarations, shattering in their truth, from these rebellious and despairing girls and boys who have won his affection. It is tragic. He slips in a quite personal admission: 'Had it not been that it entered my own heart through the suicide of a dear friend, I have no doubt that I would have passed by this despair, born of a world deprived of the divine sun.' And further on: 'Vicious aggressiveness is simply a frustrated thirst for love.' He denounces this world that is empty of personal relationships, and entitles his book 'The future belongs to tenderness'.

I agree, the future belongs to tenderness; but I am afraid of being misunderstood. I have just returned from the Ecumenical Institute, where they are holding a seminar on the ministry of healing in the church. I have had the pleasure of renewing my acquaintance with the Rev. Granger Westberg, who has done so much to foster a real dialogue between doctors and theologians. Naturally some of the participants gathered round us and soon I was being questioned about this book I am writing. My interpreter was a charming Polish lady, Mme Halina Bortnowska.

Suddenly she stopped translating and addressed me excitedly: 'Tenderness! Oh, how irritating it is for women constantly to be reminded that it is their mission in life to spread tenderness! Isn't that just another way of sending them back to the nursery, away from active life, on to the margins of society, a way of denying their intellectual and objective abilities, and reducing them to the minor function of comforters?' In order to try and comfort her myself, I placed the tenderness which it is permissible to express in a much more austere context.

In particular, I tried to clear up the misunderstanding. I do not deny the objective aptitudes of women any more than I consider men incapable of tenderness. We are conditioned by the contempt for tenderness which characterizes our society, and which reduces it to mawkish sentimentality, to a consoling caress, to a mere softness which is of no use to us in the harsh realities of life. Tenderness is something different. I suggest another definition: tenderness is attention to the person. That is why I have talked about the person all through this book, about the personal relationship which we must rediscover. As Erich Fromm writes: 'Modern man is alienated from himself, from his fellow men, and from nature.' No doubt this personal contact is still preserved in the nursery. It is, in fact, everywhere else that it is tragically missing; in society, in the world of work, in office, workshop, and laboratory – everywhere attention to the person is cruelly lacking. How could I speak of a mission for women in this society if they were still to be kept out of it?

The same thing happened when I spoke on this subject in Basle. The first woman who spoke in the discussion had thought that I was talking about a mission for women that thrust them once again into a different field of activity from men, away from the world of work which is the very field in which I am calling upon them to exercise this mission. No doubt I cannot avoid these misinterpretations. The problem arouses so many passions and susceptibilities. Women who have fought hard for the right to break through the sexual apartheid are only too ready to suspect me of wanting to thrust them back again, and I can understand them.

I must at least declare quite clearly that that would be exactly the opposite of the truth. The mission for women of which I am speaking here concerns all women, each in her own place: whether married or unmarried, at home or at work, or both, they have the same mission, the reinstatement of the primacy of persons over things. It is in public life and in the cultural sector that this primacy is disregarded most. Hence the importance of women breaking into those sectors, and having their authority in them respected.

The same is true in politics, where personal relationships rarely exist between those who confront each other in partisan arguments which remain sterile for lack of mutual knowledge and understanding. A former member of one of our governments confided to me that it was with two of his political opponents that he got on best.

The truth is that to establish a truly personal relationship is not easy; and that it is even more difficult for men than it is for women, because they are afraid of the emotion involved in opening one's heart to another person. It is possible for us men to go on discussing among ourselves the most interesting professional, technical, or academic problems, without revealing any of the things that really preoccupy us. It is a friendly, pleasant, and even attractive trait. But think of all that is being covered up – the mutual judgments, the secret hurts, the jealousies, the mental reservations, the fears and rancours that are hidden behind that conventional façade.

Among women there often arises a feeling of unease, of hurt pride. We put it down to their being more susceptible than men. Really, however, it is because they are more personal and more intuitive; their emotions are always on the alert; they are more ready to make veiled criticisms, and more sensitive to such criticism when they are the targets of it. In short, there are two territories – that of objective, abstract ideas, which can become the subject of fierce argument without much risk of anyone getting hurt, and the realm of personal problems, heavily loaded with emotion. To the latter, men are too willing to turn a blind eye. They are careful not to cross the frontier between the two territories.

I had occasion to observe this only last month, in France. I took part in a reunion with several old friends from the Medicine of the Person Group. It was lovely. Imagine it – for years we had worked closely together, we knew all about the importance of personal contact, we opened our hearts to each other, we thought we knew each other through and through. And yet, perhaps for that very reason, I felt that our discussions were in the air, that we were giving ourselves over to a kind of euphoria, and not getting down to personal realities. We had scarcely ventured at all over the frontier to which I have referred.

Then, all of a sudden, the women spoke up. Women who even in a privileged company such as that remain much too discreet – a fact which I had never noticed before! Several in the group, when their turn came to speak, had confined themselves to saying modestly, 'Oh, I haven't much to add to what my husband has said.' Then suddenly it happened – all seven women spoke at length, one after the other, throughout the morning.

It was Simone Scherding who opened the floodgates. It was Mothers' Day in France, and she spoke of the emotion of woman's supreme experience, the joy in childbirth, which no man can ever know. You will see that we have come back to the theme I referred to in Chapter 11, when speaking of the books by women writers, namely the experience of childbirth, which truly has, as Claude

Maillard puts it, an 'initiatory value'. It was not referred to again during the rest of the morning, but it had proved to be the magic wand that opened the door!

I called it the opening of the floodgates just now, but even that expression is too feeble to describe what was happening. It was as if some great dam in the mountains had burst, and that all the water in the lake behind it was sweeping down into the valley. How many personal problems there are in every family! Truly, women have better eyesight than men in this matter. How we listened to them! We were glancing at each other as they spoke. It was as if they had said to us, 'This is the reality of life, which you either cannot or will not see.' While one of them was detailing all the problems of her household, her children and her grandchildren, my neighbour leaned towards me and whispered: 'And to think that I thought that that was a family with no problems!'

In fact my whole career has taught me – and there it was plain for all to see – that women are much more realistic than we are, and much more courageous in facing up to the problems to which we are only too willing to shut our eyes. Many a time it has been Nelly who has opened my eyes, both to our own problems and to those of our friends, of my colleagues, and of my patients – but mostly to my own. And not only she, but all the many women with whom I have been in dialogue in my consulting room.

Why is it that we pay so little attention to what women have to say? Why do we expect nothing more from them than agreeable trivialities? Can it be that the problems they perceive are too painful and too difficult to solve, compared with the technical problems which excite us men? Do you not think that there are such problems in every enterprise, in every department of social and political life, and that there too women ought to be listened to more than they are? It is because there is a conspiracy of silence, because no one talks about emotional problems, that so many of our contemporaries feel the heavy solitude of which sociologists such as David Riesman are talking nowadays.

There is a new kind of solitude that is specific to our over-technical, over-organized, over-massive Western civilization, a solitude in the mass. Even in our mass leisures we can be terribly lonely. Women suffer more than men from this modern form of loneliness. That, I imagine, is the main reason why there are more women than men in the psychotherapists' consulting rooms.

Married women like those I have described, whose husbands talk only about facts and ideas, never about feelings, addressing themselves only to the intellect, not the real and emotional being, the person. But also, and with even more justification, countless unmarried women, who need above all to find deep, firm masculine friendships in their social lives, but feel that they are looked upon by men as nothing more than work-machines, without any regard for themselves as persons – except for the lustful glances against which they have to defend themselves.

With my male outlook, and like many other psychotherapists, I have tried for a long time with little success to awaken in such women an ambition to stand on their own feet, not only to accept their solitude, but to come to terms with themselves, to take pride in their own autonomy. Women, however, despite the attitude they may adopt, do not aspire so much to autonomy as to a successful, stable, profound relationship; not to dependence, as is sometimes said, but to a relationship in which they will find true freedom. France Quéré has made the point: for a man, liberty means autonomy, whereas a woman experiences it only in successful relationship.

Therefore, instead of inviting women to accept this solitude, it seems to me to be preferable to ask them to cure *our* solitude, to bring warmth back into our frozen world of objectivity, to give our mechanized society a soul. That is the mission which I propose for women, and it seems to me that it can provide a worthwhile aim for the women's movement. This is what that militant feminist, Claire Evans-Weiss, is saying in her book *Le défi féminin*, a book which is a spiritual testament, since she undertook the writing of it on learning that she was suffering from an inoperable cancer.

She tells of her youth in the days of the first feminist victories. The ambition of a young woman like her was to be 'the first woman to ... As her father was a test pilot, she wanted to be 'the first woman to fly round the earth via the north and south poles'. Then she tells of how different her life turned out to be, though no less adventurous since she encountered, just after the war, the spiritual movement founded by Frank Buchman, to which I owe as much as she does.

Then she reflects upon the meaning of feminism: 'Ask the leaders of these movements,' she writes, 'from what it is they think they are liberating their sisters, and they will never be at a loss for a reply. The list is long and varied: from male exploitation, from economic exploitation, from slavery to taboos, from the servitudes of pregnancy, the monotony of house-work, sex discrimination, and much more besides.' – 'Free from what?' she adds, 'is easy to answer. But free *for* what is not so easy.'

That raises the question of the ultimate goal of the feminist movement, and the question of a 'second wind' which might give it new strength if the liberty it claims for women were to make it possible for them to undertake a historical mission. She writes: 'What if we women decided first what is the goal for which we want to be free, a goal which will project us beyond ourselves and our limitations, a goal directly related to the contradictions of this present world?'

That is the spirit in which I have written this book, thinking that in really seeing what is missing in our Western world, women may be able to distinguish more clearly what we can expect from them in exchange for what they expect of us. Their essential claim, I think, is to be recognized as persons. That implies the advent of a 'civilization of the person', in which technological progress will itself find its meaning in the service of the person.

What is the person, then? It is man as God created and wanted him to be; man in his totality and his unity, in his 'globality', as Dr Stark says, body, mind, and spirit. It is also man, not in isolation, but in relationship, in relationship with his fellows, with nature, and with God, for it is in personal relationship that he becomes a person.

Finally, the person is man and woman together, and not man alone. In his fine book *Le désir et la tendresse*, Eric Fuchs recalls the saying of Jesus, 'Have you not read that the creator from the beginning made them male and female ...?' He explains that in Jesus' language the expression 'from the beginning' does not only express anteriority in time, but 'signifies symbolically the primal will of God', his 'founding will'. Thus the foundation of the person – the 'image of God' who is himself the person *par excellence*, and the harmony and fullness implicit in the notion of the person – is the indissoluble complementarity of man and woman. For procreation? – Certainly, when he says to them, 'Be fruitful, multiply, fill the earth ...' But he goes on, 'and conquer it' (Gen. 1.28). Is not the whole of history and civilization embodied in that command? Man and woman are to build the world together – not a masculine history filled only with the vicissitudes of an endless race for power, nor a masculine civilization which asserts the priority of things over persons.

List of Works Quoted

Aesop, *Fables,* trs S.A. Handford, Penguin Classics, Harmondsworth 1970

Aron, Jean-Paul and Perrot, Michèle, 'A propos du destin de la
femme du XVIe au XXe siècles', in Sullerot, *Le fait féminin,*
(q.v.)

Bergson, Henri, *The Two Sources of Morality and Religion,* trs
R.A. Audra and C. Brereton, Macmillan, London and New
York 1935

– *Creative Evolution,* trs Arthur Mitchell, Macmillan, London
1911

Bernheim, Nicole-Lise, 'Les pommes de terre', *Les Femmes
s'entêtent,* Gallimard, Paris 1975

Bertherat, Thérèse, and Bernstein, Carol, *Le corps a ses raisons,* Le
Seuil, Paris 1976

Buber, Martin, *I and Thou,* trs R. Gregor Smith, T. & T. Clark,
Edinburgh 1966

Cardinal, Marie, *Les mots pour le dire,* Grasset, Paris 1975

– *Autrement dit,* Grasset, Paris 1977

Carson, Rachel L., *Silent Spring,* Houghton Mifflin, Boston 1962,
Hamish Hamilton, London 1963

Collange, Christiane, interviewed by Jacqueline Baron in *La Suisse,*
8 March 1979

– *Madame et le management,* Tchou, Paris

– *Je veux rentrer à la maison,* Grasset, Paris 1979

Daudet, Léon, *The Stupid Nineteenth Century,* trs Lewis Galan-
tière, Payson and Clarke, New York 1928

Dawkins, Richard, *The Selfish Gene,* Oxford University Press,
Oxford 1976

Delumeau, Jean, *La peur en Occident XIVe - XVIIe siècles,* Fayard,
Paris 1978

Descartes, René, *Discourse on Method*, trs J. Veitch, Open Court Publishing Co., Lasalle 1977

Dolto, Françoise, in conversation with Gérard Sévérin, *L'Evangile au risque de la psychanalyse*, Jean-Pierre Delargue, Paris 1977

Domenach, Jean-Marie, *Emmanuel Mounier*, Le Seuil, Paris 1972

Doolittle, Hilda, *Tribute to Freud*, Carcanet Press, Oxford 1971

Dröscher, Vitus B., *They Love and Kill*, trs J.V. Heurck, Dutton, New York 1976, and W.H. Allen, London 1977

Dürckheim, Karlfried Graf v., *Méditer – pourquoi et comment*, Le courrier du livre, Paris 1978

Eisenberg, Léon, 'La répartition différentielle des troubles psychiatriques selon le sexe', in Sullerot, *Le fait féminin* (q.v.)

Ellul, Jacques, *The Betrayal of the West*, trs M.J. O'Connell, Seabury Press, New York 1978

Enjeu, Claude, and Save, Joana, 'Structures urbaines et réclusion des femmes', *Les Femmes s'entêtent*, Gallimard, Paris 1975

Ernst, Dr Sieger, *Europäische Aerzteaktion*, World Federation of Doctors who Respect Human Life, Postfach 1123, D-7900 Ulm/Donau

Evans-Weiss, Claire, *Le défi féminin*, Caux, Switzerland 1977

Fabre, J.-H., *Souvenirs entomologiques*, Delagrave, Paris 1923

Franceve, 'Le travail des femmes dans un hypermarché', *Les femmes s'entêtent*, Gallimard, Paris 1975

St Francis of Assisi, *Little Flowers*, Sheed and Ward, London 1979

Freud, S., *Beyond the Pleasure Principle*, trs James Strachey, Hogarth Press and Institute of Psycho-Analysis, London 1950

Friedan, Betty, *The Feminine Mystique*, Penguin Books, Harmondsworth 1965

Fromm, Erich, *The Art of Loving*, Unwin Books, London 1957

Fuchs, Eric, 'Chance et ambiguité de la famille selon l'Evangile', *Bulletin du Centre protestant d'études*, Geneva, September 1977

– *Le désir et la tendresse*, Labor et Fides, Geneva 1979

Gander, Dr Joseph, 'Die Entwicklung der Medizin von Virchow zu Tournier', *Civitas I Jahrg.*, No. 9

Gelly, Jacqueline, *Moi, Claire*, Stock, Paris 1977

Groult, Benoîte, *Ainsi soit-elle*, Grasset, Paris 1975

Halimi, Gisèle, *La cause des femmes*, Grasset, Paris 1973

Halsell, Grace, *Soul Sister*, Fawcett, Greenwich, Conn. 1969

Haynal, André, 'Le sens du désespoir', *Revue française de psychanalyse*, Presses Universitaires de France, Paris 1 Feb. 1977

Héritier, Françoise, see Sullerot, *Le fait féminin*.

Jacob, François, *The Logic of Living Systems*, trs B. Spillman, Allen Lane, London 1974

Janov, A., *The Primal Scream*, Abacus Books, Sphere Books, London 1973

Jaspers, Karl., *Great Philosophers*, trs R. Manheim, Harcourt Brace, London 1975

Jung, C.G., *Modern Man in Search of a Soul*, trs Dell and H.G. Baynes, Routledge, London 1933

Koupernik, Cyrille, see Sullerot, *Le fait féminin*

Kübler-Ross, Elisabeth, *Les derniers instants de la vie*, Labor et Fides, Geneva 1975

– 'Rencontre avec les mourants', *Revue française de Gérontologie*, Paris, No. 73ff.

Lack, D., *The Natural Regulation of Animal Numbers*, Clarendon Press, Oxford 1954

Laslett, Peter, 'Le rôle des femmes dans l'histoire de la famille occidentale', in Sullerot, *Le fait féminin* (q.v.)

Leclerc, Annie, *Parole de femme*, Gallimard, Paris 1974

– *Epousailles*, Grasset, Paris 1976

Le Garrec, Evelyne, 'Les camarades et la grève des femmes', *Les femmes s'entêtent*, Gallimard, Paris 1975

Lescaze, Marie-Claire, 'Si les maris et si les femmes …', Interview with Dr Tournier, *La Vie Protestante*, Geneva, 26 August 1977

Levy-Valensi, Eliane Amado, *La communication*, Presses Universitaires de France, Paris 1967

Lortz, Joseph, *Histoire de l'Eglise des origines à nos jours*, Payot, Paris 1956

Maillard, Claude, *Le présent des femmes*, Robert Lafont, Paris 1978

Martin, Eric, 'Ne pas confondre médecine et mécanique', *La Suisse*, 23 October 1977

Maynard Smith, J., *The Theory of Evolution*, Penguin, London 1975

Miller, Henry, *Sexus*, Panther Books, Granada Publishing Ltd, St Albans 1970

Millet, Kate, *Sexual Politics*, Virago, London 1977

Monod, Jacques, *Chance and Necessity*, trs A. Wainhouse, Fontana, London 1974

Moody, Raymond, *Life after Life*, Stackpole Books, Harrisburg, Pa 1976

Morgan, Marabel, *The Total Woman*, Spire Books, Revell 1975, and Hodder & Stoughton, London 1975

Mottu, Philippe, *Le serpent dans l'ordinateur*, La Baconnière, Neuchâtel 1974

Mounier, Emmanuel, 'Refaire la Renaissance, manifeste', *Esprit* No. 1

Nanchen, Gabrielle, interviewed by J.-M. Bonvin with comments by Georges Plomb, *La Suisse*, 3 March 1979

Nin, Anaïs, *In Favour of the Sensitive Man and Other Essays,* Harcourt Brace Jovanovich, New York, and W.H. Allen, London 1978

Nodet, C.H., 'Position de saint Jérôme en face des problèmes sexuels', *Etudes Carmélitaines*, 1952

Oraison, Marc, *Au point où j'en suis*, Le Seuil, Paris 1978

Pascal, Blaise, *The Pensées*, trs J.M. Cohen, Penguin Books, Harmondsworth 1961

Péguy, Charles, *Oeuvres en prose*, Gallimard, Paris 1957-9

Pernoud, Régine, *Pour en finir avec le Moyen Age*, Le Seuil, Paris 1977

Perrein, Michèle, *Entre chienne et louve*, Grasset, Paris 1978

Plato, *Phaedo*, trs and notes by D. Gallop, Clarendon Plato Series, Oxford University Press, Oxford 1975

Plutarch, *On the Delay of the Divine Justice*, trs A.P. Peabody, Little, Brown & Co., Boston, Mass. 1885

Portmann, Adolf, 'Mensch und Natur', *Die Bedrohung unserer Zeit*, Friedrich Reinhardt, Basle

Quéré, France, *La femme avenir*, Le Seuil, Paris 1976

Ricoeur, Paul, 'Vraie et fausse angoisse', *L'angoisse du temps présent et les devoirs de l'esprit* (Rencontres Internationales de Genève), La Baconnière, Neuchâtel 1953

Riesman, David, *The Lonely Crowd*, Yale University Press, London 1950

de Rougemont, Denis, *L'avenir est notre affaire*, Stock, Paris 1978

Rougier, Stan, *L'avenir est à la tendresse*, Editions Salvador, Mulhouse 1978

Sartre, Jean-Paul, *Existentialism and Humanism*, trs P. Mairet, Methuen, London 1948

Sergy, Denyse, 'Lettre ouverte à l'homme de ma vie', *Réalités*, Paris

Spitz, René A., *The First Year of Life*, International University Press, London 1965

Stark, André, 'Expression corporelle et globalité', Doctoral Thesis in the Medical Faculty of Geneva, unpublished

Sullerot, Evelyne, *et al., Le fait féminin*, Fayard, Paris 1978

Teilhard de Chardin, Pierre, *The Future of Man*, Fontana, London 1968

Tournier, Paul, *The Meaning of Persons*, trs Edwin Hudson, SCM Press, London 1957

Van der Meersch, M., *Bodies and Souls*, trs Eithne Wilkins, Pilot Press, London 1948

Vergote, Antoine, *Dette et désir*, Le Seuil, Paris 1978

Vilar, Esther, *The Manipulated Man*, trs Eva Borneman, Abelard-Schuman, London 1972

– *Pour une nouvelle virilité*, Albin Michel, Paris 1977

Vittoz, Roger, *The Treatment of Neurasthenia by Means of Brain Control*, trs H.B. Brooke, Longmans, London 1913

Weizsäcker, Viktor von, *Der Begriff der Allgemeinen Medizin*, Enke, Stuttgart 1947

Westberg, Granger E., *Minister and Doctor Meet*, Harper & Row, New York 1961

Witelson, Sandra, 'Les différences sexuelles dans la neurologie et la cognition: implications psychologiques, sociales, éducatives et cliniques', in Sullerot, *Le fait féminin* (q.v.)

Wynne-Edwards, V.C., *Animal Dispersion in Relation to Social Behaviour*, Oliver & Boyd, Edinburgh 1962

Yamaguchi, Minoru, *The Intuition of Zen and Bergson*, Herder Agency, Tokyo 1969

Zazzo, René, 'Quelques constats sur la psychologie différentielle des sexes', in Sullerot, *Le fait féminin* (q.v.)